THEATRE FOR THE 98%

THEATRE FOR THE 98%

Maxine Klein

SOUTH END PRESS

Library of Congress Catalog Card No. 77-86334
ISBN: 0-89608-000-5 paper
0-89608-001-3 hardcover

Photo credits: Boston University Photo Service, Susan Bruyn, and
Photographic Laboratories, University of Minnesota

Format for *Touch Kiss* conceived by Cynthia Gregg Whitman

Cover Design and inside graphics by Pat Andreotti

Printed in the U.S.A.

Published by
SOUTH END PRESS, BOX 68, ASTOR STATION, BOSTON, MA 02123

CONTENTS

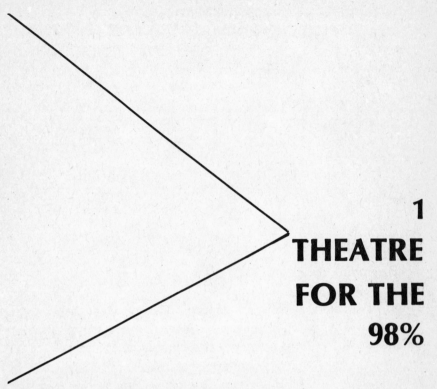

1
THEATRE
FOR THE
98%

There is a phenomenon in today's world that is worth taking a close look at.

It is inexpensive
    idealistic and
    pragmatic.

It ignores class lines.

It affirms people's worth.

The phenomenon is the people's movement. And it is *happening everywhere*. Just look around:

wherever there is an establishment with its rigidly systematized
                            "rational"
                            authoritarian
                            elite-exclusive behavior

there appears the people's group with its democratic
                            spontaneous
                            for-the-people ethic.

These people's groups are usually poor
                unusually dedicated and
                more than unusually resourceful.
In practical terms, they take whatever they can and, for the good of the
people, they "make do." And like David with his slingshot, these ready
improvisators frequently find to everyone's amazement—including
their own—that what they have is quite enough.
A trip through the People's Yellow Pages reveals the extent of the
people's movement. It's in

law	education	publishing
commerce	politics	gardening
medicine	prisons	roofing
restaurants	religion	living arrangements

And it's in theatre.
Just beginning really.
But the beginning is solid.
It has been said that children invariably live out what their parents
neglected. The parental neglect which the developing people's
movement in theatre is living out is a communal contract.

This is a contract which is built on the assumption that all people, not
                just those select few "artists" up there on the estab-
                lishment stage, have a genuine artistic sensitivity
                and that there is much good pleasure for all to be
                had from expressing that sensitivity.

This is a contract which says that the lives of all people (not just the
                high and mighty and pretty) are interesting, valu-
                able, and worthy of being the subject of theatre.

This is a contract which says that instead of the psychological or sex
                or power trip of one person, the life and welfare of
                the community is the greatest cause for celebration.

How much validity does such a communal contract have for today's
society? Well, just take a look at that most respected—and establishment—*Journal of the American Academy of Arts and Sciences,
Daedulus:*

> ...domestically the United States is becoming a *communal*
> society.[1]

It is a communal people's theatre for our emerging communal society that this book proposes to explore. And first and last, by design and execution, the exploration will be practical.

    For sad to say
    like most classrooms, congressional halls,
    and research centers, most books in this country
    are not a preparation for doing: they are a
    substitute.

Such books follow their own tail 'round in a circle.
They identify a problem
    analyze the problem to their own "objective"
        safe and
        scholarly content until
they *theoretically* resolve the problem.
Then comes the result of such theoretical resolution:
    a federal establishment sigh of relief is heard.
    This even though, or perhaps because of, the fact
    that no real action toward the real problem was
    proposed.

So the earth's circle
with its real and growing problems
continues inviolate
as the theoretical books whirl 'round
    hot air borne
never touching dirt until they land in the dust of a fifth floor,
metropolitan library, safely bound
    gagged and
    catalogued.

To avoid that stasis
    that promised land which most formal education prepares
        us for
    that land where you never have to put your money where
        your mouth is
here is a possible
    useful
    workable handbook
    for people who want to do people's theatre.

Devoted to passion and practice,
the book provides ideology

history
scenarios
plays
training
populist treatment of traditional plays and
source and resources for this theatre of

by and
for the
people.

As you read the proferred ideas
know that all have been tested by real people

in the real world
to real effect.

And, like the theatre it describes, the book itself is not exclusive.
It is inclusive. The democratic premise of the book is that there is a
people's theatre which exists
or can be made to exist for anyone, anywhere, who has the will to do it.
So, while this is obviously a book which directors

teachers
students and
actors in people's theatre

can use to practical advantage,
it is also a book for physical education people

parks and recreation people

as well as for people
who want to do theatre in community centers

hospitals
factories
homes for the long-living

as well as for people
who want to do theatre just about anywhere else you might imagine.

Now this book will take into account that
not everyone can or wants to do
every kind of people's theatre.
So some scenarios and plans of action will be specifically ear-marked
as possibilities for people's theatre in schools
                                    prisons
                                    homes for the long-living
                                    etc.
Of note, no scenarios will be ear-marked for use by establishment
theatres because there obviously is not a pressing demand by the estab-
lishment for people's theatre.
But then neither is there much of a demand
by the people
for establishment theatre.
Only about 2% of them go
with any regularity.
So, whatever else this book is
it is a plan of theatre action which proposes to serve the other part of
the population not being served by establishment theatre:
This book is about theatre for the 98%.
Call it the other theatre.
Call it our theatre.
Call it political theatre.
Call it poor theatre.
Call it democratic theatre.
Call it downtown theatre.
Call it makin' do.
Whatever you call it, it is a people's theatre.
And that's name enough and reason enough for any theatre.
So let's go with it and get on with it.

FOOTNOTES
1. *Journal of the American Academy of Arts and Sciences, Daedulus,* "Toward the Year 2000," summer, 1967, p.977.

2
THE
ESTABLISHMENT
AND ITS
UPTOWN THEATRE

Personally, socially, economically, environmentally, politically—however you view it, whatever you call it—we the chosen, we who have everything are falling apart. In this last decade the number of patients receiving psychiatric care has doubled (we can but imagine the number needing but not having the money or sense of self-worth to seek such care); the divorce rate has risen at a relentless pace since the 50's, reaching as high as 70% in some West Coast communities; alcoholism—the nation's most persuasively "packaged and pushed" addiction—has been steadily rising since the 50's; and suicide is now the fifth leading cause of death for people between the ages of fifteen and twenty-four.

Clearly the individual in this society is either being threatened by or is actually living through crisis after crisis. However, since our society's buying and selling dynamic and its consequent life style are built on the *cult of the individual*, such talk of personal dilemmas, however painful, is at least understandable. It even becomes luxurious in its comprehensibility when we try to understand the global realities which our personal crises feed in and out of.

Our egocentric American mind is quite at sea when asked to consider how and to what extent our destiny is tied up with the destiny of all people. Why should we, the *winners*, have to cope with the oil and food crises; the overpopulation, under-employment, inflation crises; the crisis of minority peoples and underdeveloped nations demanding self-actualization; the crisis of the bipolar world of the 50's giving way to the multipolar worlds of the 70's; the crisis of the Coca Cola and Chase Manhattan cartels amassing more power than the favored nation that spawned them.

These are the stunning, numbing, dumbing crises. These are the crises that make us all souls on ice. And as we surge forward towards our newest, desired, and deserved acquisition the ice underfoot gets thinner and thinner, and we begin to be aware that should we fall through, we won't even be allowed to drown; we'll choke to death on Atlantic Richfield's latest spill of radioactive waste.

But what has this personal-global crisis to do with theatre? Well, obviously very little—at least with establishment theatre. Or, more precisely, establishment theatre has nothing to do with it. Even though we have it on reliable authority that theatre ought to hold up the mirror to its age, our theatre turns a deaf ear to our national and global crises and listens to other, more commercial advice. Today's mirror is rendered opaque; today's voice is silenced. And in that silence, as in all silence, there is a terrible complicity.

Now, undeniably, there are a few in establishment theatre today who are not silent. These are figures signalling us through the flames. These are people in regional theatre, in New York, in college, high school, and community theatre who do staggeringly revealing, responsible and courageous work. But there are not enough of them.

Responsible artists, politicians, and scientists have warned us that unless we change our present course of action, this civilization could perish in as few as three decades. In the face of such warnings, what does most of our theatre do most of the time? More or less what it has always done all the time which is more or less nothing. Broadway continues to churn out its endless, apparently self-regenerating supply of musical comedies, revivals from yesteryear: Debbie Reynolds vehicles, mannered imports from England, and sex comedies, sex reviews, and sex dramas.

The less sexy, more ambitious regional theatre still does its predictable potpourri: one or two selections from its hit parade of the 17th century; at least one third-rate play by a first or second-rate dramatist; any American play from 20 or 30 years ago; then, to round out the season and prove they are located in the mainstream of

American culture, they will include a new play, preferably a musical, hopefully Broadway bound.

In most community theatre, almost any old, bad play is apparently a fun play to do; old, bad melodrama from around the turn of the century; old, bad comedies from the 30's and 40's; and old, bad musicals from almost any old time.

The "avante-garde" theatre either camps it up or does plays so erudite that no one knows what's happening—or cares. Their guiding lack of principle seems to be that there must either be a character like super-cunt (who recently graced one of the off-off's titillations) or the play must be art for art's sake, which means obscurity for the in-group's sake, which means that someone on the *Village Voice* is sure to like it.

In college theatre with its eclectic, "give 'em a bit of everything, so that no one need have a view of anything" policy, almost any of these aforementioned season's—seasonless—offerings will serve (with the possible exception of super-cunt). Five or six year-old Broadway glitter; first to third-rate Shakespeare; the Wilder-O'Neill staple; old, bad plays from the good old days—any and all are fair pedagogical game for a season's educational smorgasbord.

If there is a common guiding principle to these seasons, it seems to be "safety first." But in all that apparent safety there is real danger. The danger is not only to the life of the theatre in that less than 2% of the people in this country ever set foot inside it. The danger lies more tellingly in the quality of life and spirit such theatre grows out of and projects. Some small incandescent part of it is beautiful and ennobling, courageous and meaningful. Some of it is everything that theatre could-should be. But too much of it is not. Too much of the outpouring from these decent establishment theatres is, on one level or another, indecent.

Too much of this theatre shows women as half-men; whores; sexy-secretary types; as fulfilled mothers or unfulfilled careerists; as ball breakers; as nervous, insecure, too scrawny or bulbous and (unfortunately for the guys) incapable of fending for themselves; or as funny, frivilous, zophtically edible and (fortunately for the guys) incapable of fending for themselves.

Too much of this theatre shows homosexuals as "bitchy"clothes horses. Too much of this theatre shows lesbians as rock-eating mutants. And too much of this theatre treats both groups as erotic deviants, themselves, and therefore as erotic diversions for their audience.

Too much of this theatre treats the aged and insane as a marginally human species whose principal value lies in the commercial fact that their eccentricities provide comic diversion for their younger, certifiably saner audience.

Too much of this theatre shows any politically committed person to the far left of the establishment paradise to be either imminently corruptable by the "good life," or else an unsalvageable, crazed, bomb-throwing radical.

Too much of this theatre shows Blacks as servants, pimps, pushers, or prostitutes—if it shows Blacks at all.

Too much of this theatre shows Puerto Ricans and Chicanos as grocery boys or sizzling bomb shells—if it shows the Spanish speaking at all.

Too much of this theatre shows workers as dumb and loyal, dumb and disloyal, dumb and sexy, or dumb and sexless—if it shows workers at all.

Too much of this theatre never shows Asian Americans.

Too much of this theatre never shows Native Americans.

Too much of this theatre never shows the lives that most people in this country live every day.

Instead, too much of this theatre does show—indeed is built on and financed by—the cult of the celebrity. And for those of us who *aren't,* celebrities *are,* as Eric Mann reminds us, a way of self-hate. [1]

In effect, too much of this theatre—sometimes only by default, only by virtue of the fact that it doesn't deal with anyone else—shows the patriarchal white, middle, and ruling class to be the only fully human class with all the rights and privileges their full humanity implies. The rest of us—the Blacks, Spanish speaking, the workers, the women, the insane, the aged, the poor, the Asian Americans, the Native Americans—by logical extension get the left-overs. And if every day this means slimmer and slimmer pickings, well, that's "show business."

Think it over.

When was the last time you did or saw a play showing Black people with steel-trap intelligence?

When was the last time you did or saw a play showing women as intelligent people in fulfilling command of a destiny not revolving around men or children?

When was the last time you did or saw a play showing the usefulness and wisdom of someone over 65? Over 60? Over 55?

When was the last time you did or saw a play showing the life of a homosexual or lesbian not revolving around their sex?

When was the last time you did or saw a play showing the genuine life of workers?

Equally telling, when was the last time you—as director, as actor, as technician, or publicist, or apprentice, or writer, or in whatever capacity—were vitally involved with other theatre people who examined and took responsibility for the ideas and images of your theatre offerings.

"Now wait just a minute," some are thinking, "We're not doing plays to put down women or Blacks or workers or old guys or anyone else. That happens, but only because we're being true to what the playwright saw and said. Anyway, we're not doing plays to educate; just to entertain. A little time out from the grind, an evening's escape, that's what we're about."

Think again. You're "about" more than you thought. No matter what the professed entertaining purpose, you can no longer afford to be unaware that theatre is an educational powerhouse. Theatre presents archetypes which influence our view of self and others. The inescapable fact is that when, for example, we see stage Blacks rating high in the sex, music, and crime categories but barely placing in intellectual categories, that staged view conditions our life view—*and this whether we're white or Black*. When we see stage women not valuing themselves, their work, the esteem and friendship of other women; when we only see them, time and again, hell and heaven sent bent on getting a man, this staged view influences how men and children, employers and other elite professionals view women and how women view themselves.

This same art-life double cross holds true for the picture that theatre projects of the aged, the insane, the Spanish speaking, the politicos and all up and down the spot-lit line-up of the dispossessed. Whether we will it or not, staged pictures cast their shadow, their selection and offering, over life pictures.

This awesome and far-reaching impact which theatre and other media have on the American way of life was described by a man who knew this country and its media. This man, Nicholas Johnson, former Federal Communications Commissioner of the United States, said:

> The difficulty in America today is that we have turned it all over to the big corporations. Time owns life. Our colleges, churches, foundations, and public broadcasting stations tend to be presided over by the same guys who decide what automobiles we'll buy and what breakfast cereals we'll eat. They publish our children's school books; they own most of the nation's artistic talent—and they have little hesitation in censoring the copy of both.[2]

Clearly, whether we get assistance from critics like Johnson or serve as our own critics, an analysis of establishment theatre reveals that its censorable copy indeed serves the interest of corporate power.

FOOTNOTES

1. Eric Mann, *Comrade George,* Harper and Row, New York, 1972, p.13.
2. Nicholas Johnson, *Test Patterns for Living,* Bantam Books, New York, 1972, p.23.

3
ANSWER

PEOPLE'S

THE

Today in the valley of total corporate control there exists a people's life-line.[1] It is comprised of people who are resisting everything about the corporate elite, from its ambiance and aerosol to its broadcast hype. And they are resisting not by dropping out but by joining up. One by one, across the country, in every line of work and defying class lines, they are building an alternative society. Call this society a people's life-line; call it collectivism; call it alternative; call it populism; call it what you want, a movement by and for the people by any name remains precisely that.

No one part of the people's movement can be understood irrespective of the whole, and taken together, it is they who are the legitimate spiritual and political heirs to the activism of the 60's. Today things may be quieter on campuses and in the street, but that's not because, as the ruling class would have us believe, the movement is dead. It only means that the spectacular agitation of the 60's which the media co-opted—only ironically to have it boomerang—has matured and transformed. It has phoenixed into the more reflective, cohesive, positive, activist people's adventure of the 70's.

Where is the movement? Everywhere. Who is part of it? Just about anyone who wants to be. There are the para-medics; para-psychologists; the underground church; architecture, law, and health collectives; the radical clerics and churches; the food cooperatives; communal living arrangements; zero population groups; the United Farm workers; Colegio Cesar Chavez; women's centers; the free schools; colleges for social change; the People's Yellow Pages; all the people's liberation movements among women, men, children, secretaries, custodians, and prisoners.

Whatever their line of work these *action-people* are out to do something about their world. And it is in their positive action thrust in the real world that the people's movement most differs from previous apathetic, beat, psychedelic and other media-inspired retreats into self. Choosing solidarity over the melancholic stasis of the solitary, these activists seize what time is left and use it, not for themselves exclusively or even primarily, but for everyone.

Claiming its role in the people's life force, this positive, long term, deep-going process, is people's theatre. With their brothers and sisters in the real world, these theatre folks set out to do something about themselves, their art, their audience, their nation, their world, and perhaps, just a bit beyond.

If their reach seems over-extended, that's because they know there is extensive work to be done, and they know it's up to them to do it. What they may lack in money, housing, funding, establishment support—and that weapon of the elite called "talent"—they make up for in work, drive, committment, energy, and, for lack of a tougher word (though maybe it's the toughest word of them all), love.

Their number, though not daily tabulated in the *New York Times*, is not small which is to admit that it is not large either but to note that it is growing—steadily and surely growing. Take Boston where I live and work. There is the People's Theatre, a working class group whose reason for being is to do plays with and for all races. So their season of plays—traditional and not—is cast absolutely irrespective of race. Black, white, tan, yellow, and gray colors may divide people outside their doors, but never inside (and maybe not so much outside, either, once the insiders leave one of their plays).

There is the Caravan Theatre whose emphasis is on doing plays which deal cogently and honestly with women. From originals like *How To Make A Woman, Focus On Me,* and *Suppose I Fall* to Brecht's *St. Joan Of The Stockyards,* they fill their season with authentic lives of women—particularly the seldom heard voices of working women. They trust these real women are everyone's concern and their substantial female and male patronage confirms their trust.

There is the Newbury St. Theatre, a cooperative of theatre workers dedicated to producing shows which analyze the social and political environment in this country. They are presently performing a dramatization of Studs Terkel's *Working*.

There is the Next Move which began its life by striking against the hierarchical injustice of the establishment theatre for whom they worked. They formed an actors' collective theatre in which working actors rather than producers control the production. They launched their first season with Howard Zinn's new play about *Emma Goldman* directed by Maxine Klein.

There is the Charlestown Working Theatre: an open organization of people working at making the theatrical experience an important part the cultural life in Charlestown. They produce plays with social themes that reflect life in their community.

And there is the very political Living Newspaper which operates out of The Redbook and performs theatre which focuses on such issues as nuclear power hazards, economics, population control, and sexist advertising.

What this quick view of Boston reveals is that (excluding college theatres) there are about as many people's theatres operating within this city as establishment theatres. And I am not talking about small elitist art theatres. I'm talking about people's theatres which have a common positive-action-thrust, a non-authoritarian working dynamic, and a utilitarian goal. It is not commerce or corporate power but people's views that speak most persuasively to and through them.

And of course there are countless more people's theatres springing up around the country. In New York city there is the Labor Theatre as well as numerous neighborhood Chicano and Black people's theatres; in Ithaca, New York there is the Ithaca Folklore Theatre; travelling in and around Appalacia there is the American Revolutionary Road Company; in the Dakotas there is Doug Patterson's Country Theatre; in Portland, Oregon there is the Family Circus; in the Western United States there are over thirty Chicano theatres, El Teatro Campesino being only the best known; in Chicago there is the Bread and Roses Theatre; and Los Angeles has its Provisional Theatre; San Francisco, its Mime Troupe.[2]

The list of such people's theatre could go on and on, but in order to find out about all of them, you have to know someone who works with them, or be *where* they happen, *when* they happen—because you are not likely to read about them in the *New York Times* or hear about them on CBS.

To show some of the inner workings and struggles, some of the pain and joy of one people's theatre, let me describe an avowedly political people's theatre of which I am artistic director: Little Flags. We are a group of twelve, about two-thirds of whom are theatre and music trained; most of whom are committed to a similar political ideology; and all of whom are dissatisfied with establishment theatre. We launched our theatre with the following statement which one of us says at the start of every performance: "We dedicate our theatre to a society free from oppression by race, by sex, by sexual preference, by age, and by class." That is a large and demanding dedication, one much easier to mouth than to do. We are not yet strong, ideological, and unified enough to defeat totally those death-isms within the group itself, to say nothing about defeating them in the world of affairs. But the dedication directs us; it challenges us; and eventually it will help determine who stays within the group, and who leaves to do other things.

In accordance with the mandate of our dedication, we chose two plays to initiate our first season, *Fanshen* and *Tania*. Both these plays deal with people's struggles against imperialism. Both are cast irrespective of race: a black and white woman together play Tania; a black man plays Fidel, a white man Che. In *Fanshen*, black and white people are the villagers in Long Bow, China, fighting against feudalism. Nothing is made of their race, it is their class struggle that is the issue. In both plays our longest living person is not foolish but wise, and her wisdom is a direct correlative of her lived experience. In both plays women embrace women and men embrace men in love and comaraderie. And it is not romantic love, or family, or personal success strivings but a dedication to the wretched of the earth that determines the play's action.

In the more obvious ways of evaluating a theatre group Little Flags has been successful. We have located ourselves in a working class area, and, while we do not play to full houses, we draw a substantial number of working class people from the area to our theatre, and they have overwhelmingly affirmed us. We pay expenses and profit-share our meager gains. We have drawn critical acclaim for our plays, our acting, and our directing. The people's network around the nation heard about us, invited us to come, and we toured over twenty states playing to thousands of people. And strong comrades in spirit like Jonathan Kozol, author of *Death at an Early Age* said, upon seeing *Tania:* "This is the most beautiful performance I have seen in ten or fifteen years. It is critical in an intelligent way of the Cuban revolution, but it is respectful, passionate, and exhilarating in a way no sensitive person can forget."[3]

Does any of this success mean that the political Little Flags will survive? No, not any of it. People's political theatre is very difficult to sustain in the United States of Commercial America. At the risk of appearing too negative, let me tell you why.

First off, for a theatre to be genuinely political, its subject matter and casting policy must address head-on people's need for power, power that is largely connected with economic structure and entrenched classes. It follows that the theatre must learn how to apply class and economic analysis to everything from one-to-one personal relationships to artistic expectations, to production content as well as to world struggle. There is a rigor demanded in that process that is both time consuming and exhausting, with not enough time left over as is needed for production problems: as even Bertolt Brecht said about his collective *Kuhle Wampe:* "Of course we expended far more effort on the organization of work than we did on the artistic work itself."[4] And Brecht began with artists who were already sympatico politically, already committed to the struggle.

A second reason political and/or people's theatres fail in this country is economics. Most operate on the basis of economic fairness. This means all money is divided equally, or according to need, or according to work expended, not according to hierarchical status. The problem faced here is not ethics but practice: there is little money to share however you slice it. Even a company like the San Francisco

Mime Troup which has been around long enough to attract a regular
and growing audience is able to give its members only around $60 a
week. Little Flags averaged $15 a week (on tour, $80 a week), and that
only for performance time, not rehearsal. As for the state and national
grant givers, money tends to come too late and too little and besides,
it's the "safe" entertainments and the elitist art-for-art's sakers that are
typically favored, not the politicos.

A third reason political theatres in this country have rough
sledding is that audiences have been educated by the media and
educational systems into avoiding political theatre. What have
audiences been educated into? A sex chase, a "star," cliche musicals, or
classics one pays attention to once every twenty minutes or so when a
famous speech comes up or a famous person comes on. Any of these,
audiences have been determined into thinking, are preferable to seeing
their own lives in the theatre, or the lives of people's heroes, or the
course of people's struggles. Now if one can lure the audience into
political people's theatre—and if the theatre is not only people-
oriented but exciting—the majority of people change their minds. But
that advertising process takes time and money—commodities that are
not the long suit of most people's theatres.

An additional reason people's theatres don't fare well in the
United States is the politicos, themselves, who stand in picket lines
demanding the rights of plumbers and maintenance workers to just
compensation for their labor, but only stand amazed when it is
suggested that theatre workers need just compensation for their labor.
Why should political theatre not be "free," we hear time and time
again. The fact that the average working day for theatre workers is 10
to 14 hours and not infrequently 20 hours; the fact that this leaves no
time left over for other jobs; the fact that, for most of us,the ticket price
is our major or only source of income; the fact that theatre workers
have mouths to feed and backs to rest and families with needs just like
all workers seem to elude political minds. Theatre workers are to
politicos what nuns are to non-Catholics: a ritualistic display prized
for their quaint passion rather than taken seriously for their total
commitment.

A final reason political theatres frequently fail is theatre workers
themselves. Anyone can take poverty for only so long and then

they begin to hanker after a regular paying job. Some go to Woolworths, some to teaching. And with some there is—as with all artists in this country—the pull of the star system. The fact that being a star is a virtual statistical impossibility does nothing to tarnish its luring luster. Not even 1% of the artist-workers will ever rise or fall to that category. Quite the reverse: 80-85% of theatre workers are unemployed all the time; 20% are underemployed most of the time; only 5% work with anything like regularity. And this most frequently comes from commercial work. Here actors, directors, technicians tie themselves to monied interests and sell their useless products by making vile caricatures of people who want products, nothing but products. Now in the United Mine Workers, were only 5-15% of the workers regularly employed, and this under degrading conditions, there would be strikes without end; but theatre workers just compete all the harder for their place in the eclipsed sun.

With all these media and poverty conditioning facts of existence, and with the necessary political struggle required, it is no wonder that the majority of political people's theatres appear—only to disappear soon thereafter. Most last around six months. If they survive that cutoff date, they may last three to five years, then disband. If they survive that period they usually last. They have gone through their struggles and disbanded and reunited enough times to give them the necessary unity and politics to last. So the San Francisco Mime Troupe, the Provisional Theatre, the Living Theatre, and El Teatro Campesino, after many struggles and endless discussions and continual desertions and a steady leftward political orientation, live. And Boston's Little Flags has made it for almost one year.

Is Little Flags worried about the prognosis? Yes. Does that stop us? Not in the least. Not for one moment. Not ever. It makes us work the harder, study the harder, try the harder, hope the harder.

For through it all, through all the poverty and ideological struggles, the criticism self-criticism, there is a feeling that sustains us, a feeling not usually allowed theatre's own in this country. It is a feeling that something is happening in a political people's theatre that cannot happen in another kind of theatre. It is a feeling that something very positive happens in a group committed, however imperfectly, to a more decent world, that could not have happened among the uncommitted. It is a feeling of being part of a larger society. We are not parasites, prostitutes, or beggars, asking of the establishment money for our lives in exchange for control over our art. We have physical and spiritual proof that we are living symbiotically with the larger people's movement.

Thus the Goddard Cambridge School for Social Change gave us free rehearsal space when needed. The Cambridge and Boston food co-ops supplied inexpensive, healthful food to those of our members who could not afford the expensive unhealthful kind. While we paid for our newspaper ads, we were afforded free advertisements in the people's network in such places as the Boston People's Newsletter, the Community Church, the Red Book Store, and the Guardian. We gave benefits for inner-city schools, Pre-Term strikers, Ella Ellison, and the Farm Workers; and Quilapuyan, the exiled Chilean singing group, advertised us at their sold out concert. The Cambridge Latin alternative school mimeographed our Latin American revolutionary songs and the Red Basement singers checked them for errors. The Mother Jones Memorial Day Care Center took care of the children of our working mothers. The Common Stock restaurant collective afforded us additional free performance space, advertised us in their bulletin and gave us a benefit dinner. The People's Bicentennial organizer, Danny Schecter, gave us free advertisements on his WBCN news broadcasts. And when the world recognized figure of the people's movement, Professor Howard Zinn, was asked in the establishment Sunday *Boston Globe* what to do in Boston, he said, "see *Tania.*"And easily as many people in the establishment as outside of it did precisely that.

All this has said to us what we need to hear—that we are not alienated from the life-force of our community: we are feeding and being fed by it.

And we take our pride and our endurance from the fact that we never, not for one instant, portray values that crush people. Quite the reverse; we are involved in our plays on the stage, as in our lives off stage, in working toward the only goal that really matters: justice for oppressed peoples. And we dare hope that we will be around for another ten years of struggle. And what power does this hope have?

Let me quote Lu Hsun who said in 1921:

> I thought: hope cannot be said to exist. Nor can it be said not
> to exist. It is just like roads across the earth. For actually the
> earth had no roads to begin with, but when many people pass
> one way, a road is made.[5]

FOOTNOTES

1. A case in point of the way the corporate structure works its control: the Radio Corporation of America owns the National Broadcasting Company. That same RCA is a major defense contractor which profits from the anti-ballistic missile system. RCA's NBC is one of the principle systems by which the public is informed of the "benefits" of the anti-ballistic missile system. Now RCA and NBC adds up to nothing for the people.
2. Other people's theatres:
   Bread and Roses Theatre in Chicago
   Carolina Reader's Theatre in Chapel Hill, North Carolina
   El Groupo Latino in Chicago, Illinois
   Free Southern Theatre in New Orleans, Louisiana
   Family Circus in Portland, Oregon
   The Provisional Theatre in Los Angeles, California
   Teatro del Barrio in Chicago, Illinois
   Teatro Desengano Del Pueblo in Gary, Indiana
   United Mime Workers in Champaign, Illinois
   Triangle Fire in New York City, New York
   El Teatro de Arte in Washington, D.C.
   Unity Theatre in Minneapolis, Minnesota
   Alive and Trucking in Minneapolis, Minnesota
   The New York Street Theatre in New York City, New York
3. This is from a letter to the cast after Mr. Kozol saw the play.
4. Bluma Goldstein, "It's a Matter of Class," in *TRA (Toward a Revolutionary Art)*, Vol. 3, No. 1, 1976, p. 5.
5. Lu Hsun, "My Old Home," *Selected Stories of Lu Hsun,* Foreign Language Press, Peking, 1963.

4
PEOPLE'S
THEATRE
OF
CELEBRATION

Plato wanted the verbal artist out of his ideal Republic. That philosopher-king knew art's potential: he knew that art which is true to its calling *changes* things. Now Plato had designed an ideal Republic, and the ideal obviously needs no change. But since we have a ways to go before we arrive at that state and are therefore in need of change, we can do with a theatre which provokes us to change.

But we also need another theatre. The existential fact of the matter is that as much as we need a theatre to goad us, we need a theatre to divert us. But we do not need that diversion via the routes of sexism

elitism

racism or gratuitous cruelty. We already have quite enough of that in and out of the theatre, thank you.

What we need is a people's theatre which affirms people and through that affirmation *energizes* us.

We need a theatre of ritual.

We need a theatre for release.

We need a theatre as an orchestrated invitation to our senses.

We need a theatre to fill our need for community.

We need a theatre which shows all of us to be fully human people

who are not enslaved	but	free
not closed	but	open
not libertine	but	liberating
not senseless	but	sensitive and sensuous

not embattling	but	embracing
not a dead end	but	evolving
not futile	but	fertile
not subservient to anyone	but	coequal with everyone.

And we need a theatre to remind us of and confirm us in nature. This must be a theatre which shows nature

not hostile	but	a haven
not raw material	but	complete in itself
not a place to be dominated	but	a dominion
not dead	but	living and feeling
not moldable	but	coexpressive.

And we need a theatre of celebration,

> for despite everything, we are still alive and we can still be happy and we can still love and laugh and create and procreate. And we can still make things better. Every day that we live *we can still make things better* and that's reason to celebrate.

The early, great civilization of the Americans, the Mayans, had a celebration for almost every month of their calendar year. Now we, perhaps, cannot equal that extraordinary confirmation of life but we can meet if part way. So look around your community, your school, church, neighborhood, work group, prison, hospital, wherever your people are located. When something happens there that might be a cause for celebration, CELEBRATE! Make a theatre piece for your community that is a joyous, communal event. It can be as goofy, as zany, as madcapish as you wish. Remember, it doesn't have to be high art, just fun.

What can give you cause to celebrate?
Almost anything!

> the opening of a food cooperative
> the closing of a MacDonald's or a Baskin Robbins

the commemoration of a birth
death
community action
new year
new voice
the starting of a community newspaper
the starting of a community action group
the building of a school
the integration of a school
and on and on.
How can you make a theatre of celebration?
Well, you might help out the environment a bit by planting a tree,
and making a little theatre out of the planting.

PLANT A TREE THEATRE
Here's how you do it:
buy a sapling (or get someone to donate one).
Make crepe paper costumes with long, flowing, green streamers.
Paint your faces to look like fruits and vegetables.
Get some musical instruments: kazoos
flutes
recorders
toy drums
guitars
combs
bottles
Announce the day.
Advertise the day.
Do the day. Here's how:
Process in an easy, joyful way to a park, a school—wherever there is a
place in your community not yet controlled by private enter-
prise that still belongs to the people.
As you process, play some songs. Sing some songs. Gather more and
more people around you. Dance a little.
When you get to the place, enact a ritual that celebrates nature and
community (perhaps from the rich lore of Native Americans).
Or dramatize an event from your own community.

Then
plant the tree.

> Make a little ritual dedication, something like:
> "as the tree grows so shall all of us: strong, free, and
> community supportive."
> Hold hands and dance around your communal tree (thereby
> giving it a little communal energy to help it grow).
> And that's enough people's theatre for one day.

Another cause for a people's celebration is *people*.
Celebrate a person who is famous, but not because of money or sex or
establishment power. Instead,

CELEBRATE SOMEONE PEOPLE-FAMOUS
IN YOUR COMMUNITY

someone who does good things for people, who is kind, who is
courageous, who is long-living, or just plain fun to be around.
Here's how to do it.
Assemble your musical instruments.
Prior to the day, on a piece of cardboard, draw the face of the
person-to-be-celebrated or blow up a photograph of him/her.
ON THE DAY, an actor holds this replica in front of her/his face (so
the real person can sit back and enjoy the whole thing).
With a fanfare of drums and flutes and other grab-bag instruments
people's music begins and the person-to-be-honored is called.
The actor-with-mask comes forward and the reason for the celebration
is announced: i.e.:

> "We honor Clarice Jones because she brings us soup when
> we're sick, because her garden is so darn beautiful, and
> because she's got a great belly laugh."

Then a short play is enacted showing the honored person doing her/his
celebrated thing.
The actor-with-mask is given a trophy (which s/he will later pass on to
the real people-celebrity: a flower, or a pear, or a book written and
inscribed by the community especially for her/him.
The actor then joins the others and they perform a finale to
commemorate the honor: a dance.

> a song
> a circus act
> whatever.

When the commemoration is over
everyone sings and dances or plays games and talks
TOGETHER
and that's another people's celebration.
Or celebrate

PEOPLE'S INDEPENDENCE OR THEIR CONTINUING
STRUGGLE FOR INDEPENDENCE

Portugal	Hawaii	Wounded Knee
Greece	Puerto Rico	Rhodesia
Boston	Attica	Cambodia
Vietnam	inner-city schools	United Farm Workers
Selma	your neighborhood	Zimbabwe

Contact a sympathetic church—or whoever might have some space.
Get someone from your community to
make fun posters and advertise the day.
Buy some brown rice
> soy sauce
> whatever vegetables and fruits are in season
> some tea.

Make a rice-vegetable dish
> fruit compote
> some tea.

At the celebration serve the simple, natural, healthful meal.
Then perform some songs for the independence being celebrated
> dances
> poetry
> short plays.

Charge a little money for the event. Take the cost of the food and give
the rest to the people whose struggle you are celebrating.
And another people's celebration has happened.
Or you might make a people's celebration theatre out of

GETTING RID OF AGGRESSION.
Gather all the pillows you can find.

Get punching bags if you have and can rig them.
Rope off a section.
Let everyone in to go "at" the pillows and bags.
Let them punch until they drop.
Then let them lie there exhausted, and listen to some music that the musicians among you can make, and have a cold drink.
Or
on a board
mount some pictures, front and rear, of people who have done bad things to your community or the world's community, and therefore deserve a kick in the behind or a tomato in the face.
Everyone throws tomatoes at the picture.
(But have a trough underneath. You can make tomato soup or juice afterwards and toast your aggressionless community.)
When there is nothing to celebrate, if you feel like it, have a

FUNK FESTIVAL.
Let people dress up in crazy stuff.
Then have a scavenger hunt
so organized that the last clue discovered
puts the group in city hall
   on stage with a symphony orchestra
   at the check-out counter of Stop and Shop.
Or make up your own funky game for your own funky people and
   celebrate the funk.
Or celebrate with a

HUMAN CARNIVAL.
Here's how to do it.
Plan your acts.
In a community newspaper and with inventive posters
advertise the day.
Admission price: should you need to raise money for yourselves to
   continue your group or for whatever needs, or should you want to
   raise money for worthy, needy friends, you can charge a small
   amount of money for the acts. (If you do charge, remember to keep
   the admission low. You want to play to the people who don't have
   money rather than to the elite who do.)

Whether or not you charge money, you will want to give some nice prizes to the people.

Give a single piece of fruit or a vegetable. One apple can bring an awareness of the beauty of that fruit in a way that buckets cannot.
Or you might get your arts and crafts skill together and make some prizes.
Or you might rummage about in your attic and find some interesting things from yesteryear.
Just don't *buy* anything. There's already enough useable but unused stuff lying around in this country. Use what is available rather than add to the pollution of the environment by buying something that manufacturers will only replenish by manufacturing more and thereby polluting more.

Now get a midway full of acts and rides. The only difference between you and a regular circus/carnival will be that everything on your midway is humanized rather than motorized. So your midway can be a little more flexible and responsive to the needs and moods of the people who came to see and play.
Here are some ideas for acts:

BOWLING
three people get on their knees
(They are bowling pins. What else?)
The game's barker hands imaginary bowling balls to people who are instructed to take careful aim and
                                    bowl.
Now the fun begins:
the pins will talk back to the bowler,
challenging him/her.
When the bowler meets the challenger and bowls
sometimes one pin will fall over right away
only to have the other two resist.

Sometimes all three will fall over
only to roll right back up again.
Eventually the bowler will get a strike and a prize, but only after much creative fun has been had.

PEEP SHOW
a man or woman lies on the ground or floor.
Still.
The barker holds her/his hands spy-glass-like around the eyes of the
viewer.
Once the spy glasses are "on" the viewer,
the peep show person begins to move on the floor
in a comic take-off of a girlie show.
Once the glasses are taken away, the dancer goes back to still.

PUT HOOP AROUND THE MIRAGE
The barker hands imaginary hoops to her/his public.
A performer extends her/his arms high over her/his head, hands
together, and begins to move like a mirage in the desert, waving,
undulating, mysterious.
The player will keep trying to get the hoop around this mirage who will
continue, mirage-like, to resist.
When the hoop finally hits the mark, the effect of it moving down the
mirage-body will signal to the player that s/he has succeeded and, of
course, a prize is forthcoming.

GET THE CLOWN
A clown taunts the audience.
The barker hands a squirt gun (real) to the audience person who wants
"at" this spunky clown.
The player will try to squirt the fast-moving clown with water. When
s/he succeeds, maybe the clown will whip out her/his own squirt gun
and shoot her/him back. (Who knows what a clown will do? And, after
all, what's good for the goose... .)

MERRY-GO-ROUND
Young women and men are moving in a circle like ponies on a
roundabout up and down, up and down with steady regularity,
and singing a carousel tune.
The barker gets riders to stand behind the ponies, taking hold of their
"manes."
The riders will then move up and down like ponies and sing along.

HAND PUPPETS
Behind a counter of old boxes, hand puppets will call out to friends

and acquaintances who pass by. When they have assembled their audience, they will sing requested tunes and tell a few jokes and sing some more.

GOLF
With careful swing a golfer uses her/his imaginary club and aims at imaginary holes. the game's barker will announce the score. Because the equipment is so cheap and space so flexible you can set up the same situation for tennis

>volleyball
>ping pong

just about any game you and your audience have a mind and imagination to play.

These circus/carnival games, plus the games you will add, give you a great people's theatre event. One that you and your audience will want to do time and time again.

Another people's theatre possibility is

SYMPHONY HALL
We all know who goes to the New York Philharmonic and the Boston Symphony. It's the people who can afford to glitter and glow. But there is another possible symphony—a people's symphony. For this one the audience doesn't need fur and feathers and the orchestra doesn't even need instruments.

Here's how to do your PEOPLE'S SYMPHONY HALL.

Get some crazy songs that uptown symphonies would never play.

Divide your people into violins

>trombones
>tubas
>kettle drums
>flutes
>pianos
>harps
>you know, the works.

Get your musical director to rehearse each section. Of course, in this symphony there are no instruments. The players mime the instruments and make appropriate sounds with their voices.

Get together and rehearse.

Then, once your musical director has decided that you have the right "symphonic sound," you're ready for your concert.

Advertise the day.

Send out ritzy invitations informing everyone that this is a white tie and tails affair.

(And describe just how the first-nighters should pin tails onto their behinds.)

On the auspicious night of nights

the wild conductor enters on roller skates.

The symphony starts, grandly,

but at any moment,

Someone hits a bad note and from off stage is thrown a wet rag which lands in his/her face or someone comes on with a cream pie and "pow!"

During a most dramatic part of the song a trombonist takes out a magazine, a violinist starts shooting dice, a cellist studies a racing form.

Midway through, a kettle drummer starts eating lunch.

A flutist falls asleep, snores, and falls off his/her chair.

The celebrity soloist keeps making her grand entrance only to be told time and time again, "not yet."

Three or four times during the symphony all the players fall asleep at one time and the conductor announces the olio acts.

1. THE FAMOUS DOG ACT

A neighbor's dog (one that a lot of people in the audience will recognize) is led on stage. The dog stands there for two or three minutes and is led off. The resounding applause will wake up the sleeping symphony and they'll resume playing.

2. THE MISS TO END THEM ALL

In a tribute to all the Miss America et. al. contests, Near Miss comes on stage. She brings with her a floor lamp with four bulbs. She plugs in the lamp (you may need a lot of extension cords or a battery pack). Next, Near Miss will "play" the lamp. To recorded music Near Miss, at appropriate musical moments, turns on lights;

> sometimes one
> sometimes two
> sometimes in a burst of wild creativity
>> she will turn on all four lights
>> in varying successive orders.

The song ends, applause once again begins the symphony.

3. THE FRUIT OF THE LOOM

A respected politician will come out to give a speech. Tomatoes will be passed out in the audience. The politician will frequently relay famous promises that were made by well-known politicians but never kept.
i.e.

Lyndon Johnson's promise not to escalate the war in Vietnam

Nixon's promise that he was not a crook

Ford's promise to end inflation

Carter's promise that his administration would help the poor

local politicians' promises to end crime and not to raise taxes.

Everytime such a promise is made, tomatoes are thrown; finally the spattered politician leaves, and the symphony resumes.

Eventually the symphony will conclude in a grand slam finale and your PEOPLE'S SYMPHONY ends. The audience applauds, making sure that there is a rich, sonorous bellowing of the appropriate "bravos." Then the audience gets up, taking their tails with them, and leaves. And another people's celebration theatre ends.

These are but a few scenarios for people's celebratory theatre. They are easy, they are fun, and you can put them together at a moment's notice. And know that once you do, you'll discover that a hundred more ideas will pop into your mind. Just as authoritarianism breeds a submissive spirit, creativity breeds a spontaneously creative spirit. Ideas will come like popcorn.

So get poppin!

Of course, there may be a time when you'll want to do a longer, more detailed and developed piece: rather than popcorn you might want a seven course meal (but you still want it as spontaneous and as democratic as your popcorn). With a group of people-actors I have done such pieces. The one I will describe to you now I must have done

over 100 times

in four different cities

with countless different actors

in professional and communal settings

and with great fun on stage and off.

Because you might enjoy reading it, or doing it, or because you might learn from it how to make one of your own, here it is.

TOUCH KISS

from *Touch Kiss* by Maxine Klein

HOW to do A TOUCH KISS:

PLACE:

any place—a room
          a hall
          outside
          even, if worse comes to worse, a formal theatre.

It's best to have the audience surround the actors
so leave space around the playing area for
the audience to sit
          squat
          kneel
          lean
          stand against the wall.

SCENERY:

none
with her/his heart
          face
          body
          soul

each actor becomes by turns—a tree
                    flag
                    bowling pin
                    fish
                    merry-go-round
                    plane—whatever is called
                                        for.

PROPS:

none—all are mimed
except Miss America's skirt and mask
                        or
sometimes a flower or three.

LIGHTS:

don't need any, except normal room light.
But if you have some and want to play around
you can make the first half more somber, shadowy
the second as bright as can be.

COSTUMES:

to each her/his own—sunny
                        funny
                        fresh
                        colorful
                        rompable
                        cool
                        comfortable—people clothes.

MAKE—UP:

none
the actors use the muscles in their face
                their imagination
                their sense of fun
to transform their look into scouts
                            babies
                            chorus girls and boys
                            mobsters
                            whatever is called for.

SPECIAL EFFECTS:

a band
is not absolutely necessary—
but if at all possible, find one.

Check out your local high school or
ask a 16-year-old for a group that could use some work.
Make up music for: the mechanical dance
                       touch kiss
                       june taylor
                       syndicate kill
                       death dance
                       the kiss machines (when they go to the
                                                        audience)
                       the encore (when the audience comes to
                                                            you)
                       wherever else you want to put it.
(if you can't get a band use
records/bottles/bones/tin cans/kazoos/orchestrated voices)

NUMBER OF ACTORS:

anywhere from 10 to 50 and on up.
A **TOUCH KISS** has been performed with 10. It worked.
It has been performed with 20 and 30. It worked.
It could be performed with 100—and it would probably work best
of all (until someone does it with 200).

MATERIAL:

the play has been written as it was performed (some of the time).
The structures never varied but individual scenes changed
depending on the talent and desires of the cast and audience.
So as you get about doing it
be assured that every scene in the play has worked
in any number of public performances.
You can feel good about using all of them.
But feel equally good about changing scenes
to fit the spirit, needs, and talents of your group and audience.
Nothing is sacred in the play except
the bond of trust to be created between you and the audience.

LANGUAGE:

the language of a **TOUCH KISS** will not alienate
                                         intimidate or
                                         segregate
                                         your audience,
because a **TOUCH KISS** is basically non-verbal play.
So
perform it for and with people of many languages
                                         cultures
                                         backgrounds
                                         ages.

The "words" of a **TOUCH KISS**
are your faces
            bodies
            voices radiating strong
                         warm
                         loving energy
and those are words enough
don't you agree?

TOUCH KISS is theatre as ritual.
In some rituals, sacraments are administered.
In some, boys and girls enter adulthood.
In some, people are joined in marriage.

In this ritual
people transcend race, cultural and language barriers
and they join together with one another to be together.

And that is sufficient reason for any ritual.

Something about the history of the play.

A **TOUCH KISS** has been seen at the Guthrie Theatre, Minneapolis
at 12 inner-city schools, Minne-
apolis
at Cafe La Mama in New York
at Boston University
at 18 inner-city schools in Boston
at the Glen Lake Detention Home
in Minnesota
at the North Dakota Festival of
the Arts
at the Playhouse Theatre in Toronto
at the Martinique Theatre in New
York
at the University of Minnesota.

Here are some of the comments from audience participants.
Some are written from newspapers.
Some are written as gifts for actors in the cast.

"Made my insides more real than than my outsides."
Sally
age 8

"I think the show was good! And I liked it too! If I was in it I know it would be good. And I would like to be in it."
Rudy A.
age 12

"Only one word—LOVE. (And thanks for that love.)"
Warren
age 9

I like to be kissed— (and kiss). Smiles are lovely."
Amy R.
age 9

"I kind of like it and I kind of didn't because it was too lovely."
Larry A.
age 13

"One of the most delightful evenings of theatre presented in New York all season.... The audience is drawn into the games and the result is charming.... Forget that old saw about whistling the music when you leave the theatre. When was the last time you kissed the proprietor?"
John O'Connor, critic for
The Wall Street Journal

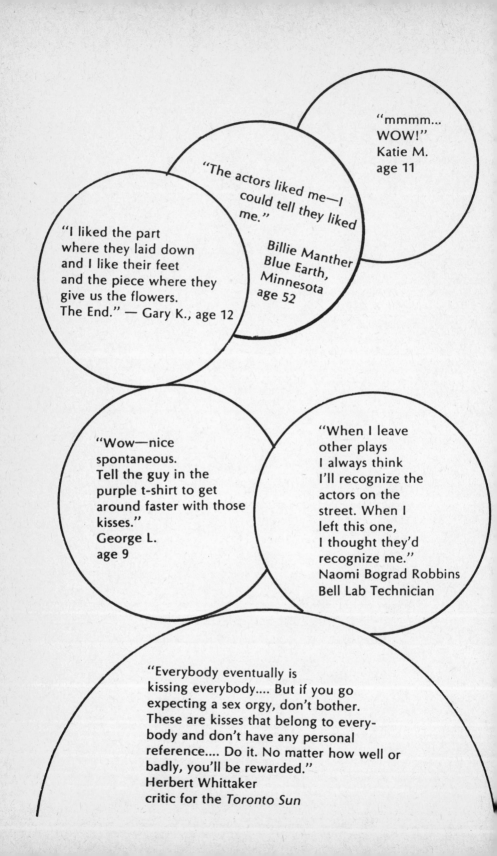

"mmmm...
WOW!"
Katie M.
age 11

"The actors liked me—I could tell they liked me."

Billie Manther
Blue Earth,
Minnesota
age 52

"I liked the part where they laid down and I like their feet and the piece where they give us the flowers. The End." — Gary K., age 12

"Wow—nice spontaneous. Tell the guy in the purple t-shirt to get around faster with those kisses." George L. age 9

"When I leave other plays I always think I'll recognize the actors on the street. When I left this one, I thought they'd recognize me." Naomi Bograd Robbins Bell Lab Technician

"Everybody eventually is kissing everybody.... But if you go expecting a sex orgy, don't bother. These are kisses that belong to everybody and don't have any personal reference.... Do it. No matter how well or badly, you'll be rewarded." Herbert Whittaker critic for the *Toronto Sun*

1. Mechanical People

In the first half of the play
the players are hollow, mechanical people:
they are walking dolls
emptied of their insides
wound up and ready to go—nowhere in a hurry.
They are comic-tragic creatures performing their daily round of
activities with the unthinking
                              unfeeling
                              uncaring precision of toy horses on a merry-go
                                                                    round.
The players enter to music.
Each is frozen into a repeated gesture pattern of
a recognizable power figure in today's society: teacher
                                                 military person
                                                 politician
                                                 pope
                                                 cheerleader
                                                 boss
In a half-organized, half chaotic traffic pattern
they pass one another.
Occasionally, as though at the mercy of a changing traffic light,
they chance to stop in front of one another
unavoidably looking at one another.
These curious confrontations do not warm their icy exterior;
instead, the confronting characters twirl with frantic numbness
as though pinned through their center to the floor beneath them.

Finally exhausted from their frantic pace
they break down.
The source of their energy suddenly turned off
the characters shake
turn plunged
        r
        o
        p
          to the floor.

2. Hollow Kiss Scenes

Following
are 8 scenes
involving
2 to 4 to 8
people
in which
human relationships
are bought and sold and sealed with a kiss.

(if you want to add
subtract } scenes
exchange
feel free
but a word of warning:
here, as elsewhere in the play,
if you're of a mind to change,
it's best to exchange and subtract scenes—not add.
Otherwise the play can get too l o n g
and part of the fun of the play is
the quickness with which it changes from scene to scene
and gets from its beginning
to its end.
So in the first section
it is probably best to cut a scene or 2
and/or if you feel like it
substitute one of your own devising.)

A note about the dynamics of these scenes.

These scenes are first done forward
from beginning to end
then in reverse
from end to beginning.
The doing of the scene in reverse
makes a satirical comment
on the forward scene.

When the actors perform the scene reversal
they should move double-time like a movie running in
reverse.

The moment preceeding the turn about
is accompanied by a kazoo sliding up the scale.
When the kazoo hits the top note the characters **freeze**
surprised! caught! in the forward movement.
Then the kazoo descends the scale
pulling the characters into the scene reversal.

Remember—in the t u r n
b a o out

the actors begin with the last action
and progress to the first. But they leave out
the significant details of the forward scene
so it takes about half as long.

NOW FOR THE SCENES.

50

a. prostitute and client

A prostitute
with a tough, sexy, facial mask
says "boom chi chi boom" in rhythm with all her actions.
She puts on her stockings
sprays under her arms
runs her hands down the sides of her body.
Suddenly a knock is heard at the door.
She wearily looks in the direction of the knock
takes out a bottle
opens it
takes a quick drink
and goes to answer the door
(probably her first customer of the day).
A military man greets her
looking properly overbearing, dull, and drooling.
He is too much for her this early.
She starts to shut the door
he offers her money
she takes it
    counts it
    and gives him a quick kiss and
    leads him toward the bed.
He responds in panting delight.

kazoo ascends
      freeze
kazoo descends

reverse: She says "ich boom boom"
siphons the spray from underarms
spits in the bottle
takes back the kiss
and pushes him toward the door.
He goes from delight
            back to greedy frustration.

b. birthday party

Twin sisters
about 5 years old
stand next to one another
giggling shyly and
watching mama approach with a birthday cake,
singing "Happy Birthday to you."
When she finishes
the girls squeal "Oh, boy!"
Mama kisses them both on the cheek with a loud smack.
The girls take a big breath
blow out the candles
pick up a huge piece of cake
lift it high in the air and
take a huge bite.

kazoo ascends
            freeze
kazoo descends

reverse: The girls spit out the cake
                inhale breath
                mutter a confused "boy o"
        as the mother backs away with the cake
                singing the words "Happy Birthday" backwards.

c. duel and curious bystander

One man gets up
takes a drink
turns around
sees 2 men—street people
stalking each other
mumbling threats under their breath.
The bystander is feigning concern
but voyeuristically is eager to see these 2 have at each other
and says "you mean...
            you aren't going to...
            you aren't..."
as he greedily looks from one to the other.
The men approach each other, suddenly
with knives aimed at each other, they
quickly veer around and
stab the middle man
who falls dead.
Smiling at the success of their conspiracy
they walk toward one another
meet
handshake
and kiss in appreciation.

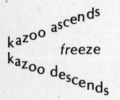

kazoo ascends
        freeze
kazoo descends

reverse: Dead man returns to his voyeuristic life.
         The street people resume their argument.

d. doctor and patient

A doctor announces to an audience of medical students
a sex transplant (in gibberish
               with just enough understandable words
               so that the audience knows what's happen-
               ing).
S/he approaches the patient
checks his eyes
and announces "He's out."
Asks the nurse for "scalpel—no, wrong one."
Then nods when given the correct one.
S/he takes it and makes a huge cross incision
clamps the skin flaps to the floor
(all is done with appropriate sounds)
looks inside
announces "He's a real mess"
and alarmed begins to pull things out of the cavity.
The patient screams and dies.
The doctor looks at him rather disgustedly and
wearily makes the sign of the cross on the patient's chest as a
final blessing
and kisses him on the forehead.

kazoo ascends
    freeze
kazoo descends

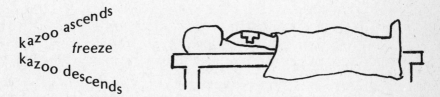

reverse: The doctor puts everything back in the patient
             in as ramshackle a way as they were taken out.
             The patient returns to life
             and awaits her/his fate
             at the hands of the professional, uncaring surgeon.

e. party

> 2 women and a man stand as if at a cocktail party
> laughing, drinking
> talking modish gibberish.
> 3 men stand up
> straighten their ties
> and enter the party.
> Upon spotting a prize catch
> each fixes his hair
> gulps down his drink
> checks his fly
> and approaches his party prey.
> As they meet they say "HELLO!"
> and kiss.

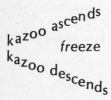

kazoo ascends
    freeze
kazoo descends

> reverse: The couple retreat from each other
>   say "Oh, hell"
>   with the disgust they had felt all along.

f. mother and baby

> A baby crawls out gurgling and cooing
> while a grumbling and unkempt mother
> is scrubbing the floor.
> The baby begins to scream and cry
> so finally the mother goes over to check his/her diapers.
> Finding them in need of change
> she unpins them
> takes them off
> (almost gagging at the odor)
> powders the baby

(who begins to gurgle happily)
and puts on a clean diaper.
She kisses him/her on the forehead
as the baby gurgles and giggles in delight.

kazoo ascends
        freeze
kazoo descends

reverse: Mother pulls off the powder
         slaps the dirty diaper back on the baby
         who screams and cries his/her anger.

g. honeymoon

Newlyweds rush into a room
kiss
and eagerly look at the bed.
With appropriate sounds
the woman first takes off

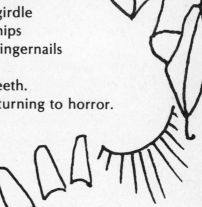

                    her eyelashes
                    breasts
                    girdle
                    hips
                    fingernails

then unhinges her knees
and finally takes out her teeth.
The man reacts in dismay turning to horror.

kazoo ascends
        freeze
kazoo descends

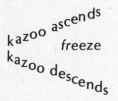

reverse: She puts everything back on.
He responds emotionally and physically
going from horror to dismay to ecstatic desire
for his manufactured woman.

h. wedding

Man and woman approach one another
shyly, expectantly, about to be married.
He is saying "Ba boom ba boom"
in rhythm with his steps.
She is sighing in rhythm with hers.
As they meet
they turn to the preacher
and happily say "I do."
He puts the ring on her finger
lifts the veil
and gently kisses her.
They turn to leave.

kazoo ascends
freeze
kazoo descends

reverse: He puts down the veil
takes back the ring.
She becomes more and more confused and
chagrined.
Both say "Do I?"
and exit.

i. plane

A well trained, trimmed stewardess
announces "Flight 747 is now boarding."
Players rise and enter the plane.

There are 2 children who rush on
laughing, talking
bumping into each other.
There are 2 Catholic nuns
praying as they go.
There is a camera happy man
and a woman who is afraid and sure she is going to
be sick at least
die at worst and
hate the flight at best.
The pilot
with all the self-assurance in the world
walks down the aisle
enters the cockpit
and announces their destination, altitude, and whatever else is
announceable.
The stewardess gaily walks down the aisle
reassuring people
greeting them
puffing up the pillows
answering questions.
This done she walks into the cockpit
transforms into a much tougher person.
Says "Hiya, Nate" to the pilot.
He says "Hiya, Shirl"
grabs her
bends her over
and kisses her.
While they are so involved
the plane collides with something.
Everyone screams
leans back
and the final sounds before the reversal
are the sounds of the woman grabbing for the sick bag.

kazoo ascends
      freeze
kazoo descends

reverse: All return to their lives before the crash and then...

3. Scouts

they transform to boy and girl scouts
proudly reciting the Pledge of Allegiance
and saluting the American flag.
While the group is involved in the pledge,
one scout reverently sings "The Star Spangled Banner"
and another transforms to the flag
which is solemnly raised
and unfurled to wave in the wind.
After the scouts complete the last line of the pledge
"with liberty and justice for all"
one scout quickly transforms to an adult with a gun.
S/he could be police.
S/he could be military.
(Look at the newspaper and decide on the basis of the
most recent slaughter which is the most appropriate.)
The adult-with-a-gun shoots all the young people.
Then s/he gives his/her gun a job-well-done kiss
and saunters through the bodies
nudging, kicking,
rolling them over to see that all are dead.
When the killer pokes the last couple of kids
they—
along with the rest of the players—
gradually rise and transform to adult military.
This militarization happens in a ghost-like way,
as though the players were not aware what was happening to
them and why.

By the transformation's completion
all have assumed tough, martial, facial masks.
They now execute a relentless march
receive the military embrace
and kiss on the cheek
and converge out
> among and
> through the audience.

4. Syndicate (younger casts may want to omit this section)

Once in the audience
the military transforms into their civilian counterparts: the
syndicate.
Each player transforms into a distinct type—
representative of the people
who make up or are accomplices of the syndicate:
> hired killers
> politicians
> show business personalities
> small business people
> big business people
(It is important here
not to do racial types.
Organized crime is a product of greed, competition, and con-
centration of power, not race.)
The syndicate boss, Eddie
positions himself center stage and
waits to hear from his gang.
They report in one at a time,
coming stealthily back onto the stage as they do.

"Hey Eddie, we got John Silky last night."

"Dope— OK in Detroit."

"Dinner with the mayor tomorrow night."

"The record company says their canaries will sing your tune, Eddie."

"Senators all agree to vote 'no'."

"The president says play dumb—he'll get you immunity."

"We got the milk machines out and the coke and candy machines back in the schools."

After Eddie has received all the reports
he whistles a command for everyone to clear out.
Just as they start to leave
Eddie stops one from leaving.
"Irving, come here."
Irving, though deadly afraid,
swaggers up to Eddie with seeming confidence.
Eddie embraces him and
gives him the kiss of death.
Eddie leaves.
The rest of the gang fire shots into Irving
who responds to each shot
in stylized, pyrotechnic dance,
reeling, gliding, crawling, stumbling, falling.
Just as Irving is about to fall the last time
he transforms to an announcer for the June Taylor dancers
and says "Thank you, ladies and gentlemen
and now for our headliners for the evening—"

5. June Taylor

The rhythm of the gun shots transforms
to the equally mad, obviously compelling rhythm
of contemporary commercial rock.
And the men and women of the syndicate transform
into June Taylor dancers.
With facial masks frozen into huge saleable smiles
and bodies poised for display
they move in a high-kicking precision dance.

As they kick and smile their way through the dance
they throw lots of kisses to the audience.
The kisses are as icy and phony and unintentionally funny
as the dancers who threw them.
The dance ends in a spiral
which lowers itself to reveal a solo Star performer.
S/he sings a song
all of whose lyrics are (like the lyrics of most popular songs)
    I love you
    I love you
    love love love you.
    love you
    love love love you.
    You you you I love.
An announcer appears saying:
    "She loves everyone of you
    as do all our contestants
    on this their day of days..."

6. Miss America

The June Taylor dancers now transform
to Miss America contestants and escorts.
The contestants embody different types of Miss Americas
(who in turn are groomed to embody
what a class society has decided its ideal women are):
    a homespun nobody
    the all-body, no-mind blond
    the sizzling, smoldering brunette
    the tempestuous redhead
    the black blazer
    the athletic amazon
    the graceful gazelle
    the sparkling starlet
Proud escorts take the contestants down the runway
the announcer calls out their name and states:
    "Miss California Cutlet

> Miss Florida Flank Steak
> Miss Louisiana Lamb Chop
> Miss Missouri Mutton
> Miss Rhode Island Rib Roast"

Each girl stands alone in her glory for a moment
then retires to the losers' column
to await the entrance of Miss America.

Finally
she enters on the shoulders of 2 men
a skirt over the men,
making her look 10 feet tall.
On her head is painted a delicious, medium rare steak.
She circles the floor throwing kisses to the audience
and generally giving out her pure delicious womanhood.

7. Flesh Market

Now the contestants and escorts transform
to the lewd flesh market that the Miss America contest really is.
Miss America stays in the center of this orgy
grotesquely smiling and throwing kisses.
The men and women go at one another
in a lewd, gross manner.
They ooze over one another
panting, grasping, clawing
but never touching.
They form tableaux
appear about to consummate their lust
when
not unexpectedly
they tire of it all
and obviously bored
walk away from one another.

8. The Dance Hall

To an ear-shattering rock song
the players walk to partners

to execute today's dance hall scene
where people dance with one another
never seeing, never touching, hardly recognizing.
Together
but not together.
The players ritualistically confirm their tragic-comic loneliness.
Dances of every style are performed: the charleston

the hand jive
the stroll
the bugaloo
the boogie-woogie
the twist
the bump

But no matter what the dance
all dancers are unresponsive
    dull
    lifeless
    listless
    barely functioning entities.

9. Death Dance

Finally the dancers collapse from sheer ennui.
One dancer is left
who is brought out of her trance-like state
by the sight of all the bodies around her.
She executes a pulsating
    frenzied
    lovely
    sad
    dance over all the bodies.

But being unable to revive them

She too collapses

and
the
first
part
of
the
show
dies.

silence
then
faintly a heart beat starts
bu-bump bu-bump bu-bump bu-bump
then tinkling music starts
everybody wakes up
rolls over
and faces center
they see
as if for the first time
each other
and the audience
they are all happy
there is no sadness
it is childlike
innocent
possible
the young man wakes up
the young woman wakes up

they dance the no touch mime

No Touch Mime

The first 2 people to be "reborn"
discover one another
shyly
slowly
naively.

These 2 people value one another
too much to touch one another casually.

They examine their own hands
feel their own bodies
exploring what they can do with them—

then they discover each other.

At first they don't know what to do with
each other but are delighted.

They run towards each other
but are afraid to touch.
They try
but can't.

So they dance together
not touching
just exploring
elbows
shoulders
heads
toes.

They chase
    play with } one another.
    dodge

Finally they kneel and
play a finger game.
The young man puts his hand too high
for the young woman to reach.
They stand and the young woman starts to
twirl around trying to reach his hand
until their fannies BUMP accidently.

Music stops...

They suddenly realize what
happened
by accident and on purpose.
They start to touch each other's face
                                    hair
                                    arms
They hold ⎤
        kiss ⎦ each other's hands.
They are delighted and
overwhelmed with joy.
(when they kiss, light twinklie music starts)

Then they start to throw kisses
to all the cast lying on the floor
who catch them in various places
(elbow, knee, hair, nose, whatever)
and throw them back.
This exchange of kisses
lets the audience know what's in store for them.

The young man and woman
now throw kisses into the audience.
The audience catches them and throws them back.
They land in legs, arms, noses, ears.
After this exchange has continued long enough
but not too long
the young woman takes a kiss she has caught
and throws it high in the air
for the young man to catch.

Symbiotic

The young man and woman
now sit on the floor and
start to play a foot game
touching
tickling
dodging.
Soon all the players join in.
The foot game is extended until
the players are touching not only one another's
feet
but the length and breadth of one another.
They move in and out of one another
enjoying one another
having fun with one another
all in a spirit of innocent child-like fun
(that adults are not immune to experiencing).

Touch Kiss

The symbiotic relationship
evolves into a song:

"A touch kiss makes a happy sound
a touch kiss makes a happy sound
a touch kiss
a touch kiss
a touch kiss makes a happy sound"
(then substitute elbow
                    foot
                    knee
for touch
and continue to sing)
The melody of the song can be easy and tuneful
so that it can be easily taught to the audience.
As a trio sings the song
the rest of the cast divides into groups,

each group performing a dance
which embodies the spirit, form and fun
of one of the touch kisses:
so one group does elbow kisses
  one hair kisses
  one toe kisses
and so on.

When everyone in the theatre is singing together
the dancers take their kisses to the audience
touch the audience's fingers with theirs,
the audience's feet with their feet.
It's fun
    frolicking—human people touching people—
    and enjoying it!
When these touch kisses have gone on long enough
but not too long
the cast returns to the playing area
sings the song one more time
and then promptly EXPLODES into the

Happy Kiss Scenes

Now comes a series of quick scenes
in which people are doing seemingly everyday activities
when suddenly—
out of nowhere—
they get a kiss.
(Remember: the kisses that will be coming in
          these scenes needn't be lip kisses.
          You've learned and taught elbow,
          toe, hair, feet kisses—
                    so use them.)

a. telephone

2 or 3 actors form a public telephone booth
complete with telephone and sliding door.
A man walks by.

The telephone rings.
He looks confused
wondering whether or not to answer a public phone.
He decides to
only to get a dial tone.
He leaves.
The phone rings again.
He runs back—
same thing—dial tone.
He gets out a dime
puts it in the phone
and dials.
The telephone answers "Operator"
and gives him a kiss.
The man gives out a happy WOW!

b. strength tester

2 people become a carnival strength tester
in the form of a bell and gonger.
A third person becomes the muscle proud contestant
who tries to ring the bell.
S/he picks up a heavy sledge hammer and
brings it down hard on the gonger.
The gonger goes up a quarter of the way
toward the bell and slides back down.
The bell ringer
confused that her/his strength didn't prevail
tries a second time with even more force
but this attempt gets even less response.
S/he now gets a gleam in her/his eye
and gently taps the gonger.
This time the gonger rises to the top
and rings the bell
and then kisses the bell ringer.
WOW!

c. piano player

3 people form a piano
with hands outstretched as keys.
A haughty, elitist begins her/his concert.
The piano kisses her/him.
S/he leaps back from the bench in surprise
returns undaunted to play again
and gets another kiss!
and jumps from the piano again!
S/he now returns to the piano for a 3rd try.
This time s/he drops the aristocratic manner
and in excited anticipation
really grooves on playing
and on the kiss that follows.
WOW!

d. fish

A girl and her companion are fishing.
First cast the girl catches nothing.
She reels in the line.
Her companion puts another worm on the hook.
The girl casts again.
This time she catches a whopper of a fish.
She reels it in
and it kisses her
and her companion
and they all dive into the water.
WOW!

e. shower

A boy transforms to a shower.
A girl walks up to her shower
and begins to bathe.
The shower gives her a kiss on the elbow.
She jumps from the shower

and thinks it over and decides
"no, the shower didn't really kiss me."
She mutters a little wistfully "too bad though"
and returns to the shower
and gets another kiss
and again bolts.
This time she decides the shower DID kiss her
and it's high time!
She runs back in
and transforms to a shower
and the 2 showers kiss.
WOW!

f. slot machine

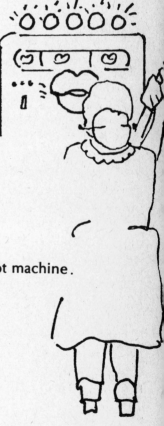

2 spry long-living women of 80
enter a gambling establishment
and go to the slot machines.
The 1st woman
gets a broken down machine
which she plays twice.
Both times it fizzles out.
The 2nd woman puts money in a machine
and wins the jackpot in the form of a kiss.
She excitedly runs to tell the 1st
(in gibberish talk)
of her unbelievably good fortune.
The 2nd woman runs to play the snappy slot machine.
Her first try is to no avail.
She mumbles about the Canadian coin
causing her trouble.
She tries again.
This time the machine sounds
as if something BIG might happen
then fizzles out.
This time the woman kicks the machine
which kicks her back.
A 3rd coin is inserted

and this time
she gets the jackpot kiss.
WOW!

g. jukebox

3 people form a jukebox.
A teeny-bopper boy dances up
to play his favorite song.
He puts in the coin
and presses the appropriate buttons.
The people go through the motions of
the inside workings of the jukebox
and begin to sing:

"I was lonely
'til one night
doing the Kiss Rock
doing the Kiss Rock
oo oo oo
When he looked at me
it was heavenly bliss rock
uh huh huh huh

Kissing's always been the rage
if you're young or old in age
Come on and Kiss Rock Kiss Rock
oo oo oo
Kiss Rock Kiss Rock"

(Of course your teeny bopper
may listen to another song. There's
nothing unchangeable or sacred about
the play except the bond you create
with the audience.)

The boy listens to the music
dancing, miming,
mouthing the words in ecstasy.

The jukebox kisses him.
WOW!

Now take the kissing pianos, fish, et al
to the audience.
Let *them* play.

(Don't fret.
They always have.)

From prisons, to formal theatres,
to schools, to detention homes,
to community centers.
Every place the play has traveled
the audience has come forward en masse
to join in the fun.

So
go out into the audience
and ask
one friend to another.

a. fish

"Do you want to fish?"
Hand him/her the imaginary pole
point out the fish
(who will be swimming about in the playing area)
tell him/her to cast and catch.
Sometimes the fish will go for the line right away.
Sometimes not.
When this happens tell him/her to cast again.
When the fish "swallows the hook"
the audience member reels it in
and gets a kiss on the cheek or forehead or hand.

b. shower

Both actors who played the shower scene
transform to showers
and walk—
in a way showers are wont to walk—
out into the audience.
With hands and arms formed like shower handles
they go up to the audience
and ask if they want a shower
pointing out,
as any self-respecting shower would,
which handles are hot water
which cold.
Instead of water however
the audience member gets a shoulder kiss!
(It's less drying for the skin than water
and much better for the heart.)

c. jukebox

The jukebox transforms to as many jukeboxes
as there were people in the scene.
The jukeboxes dance out to the audience
with 10 finger selection keys extended.
Each asks the audience to select a tune
and for their imaginary quarter
they get a real song (any one from the show)
and a kiss (any one from the show).

d. telephone

Both telephone and caller transform to a telephone
(with consideration for the public that
corporate ma bell has never shown).
Ringing
the telephone they telephone-dance to the audience.
They find someone
"there's a call for you."

The player-phone keeps ringing
until it is answered.
When the audience member says "Hello"
into the player's hand-receiver
s/he gets a telephone kiss on the ear.
(Not too loud.)

e. piano

Each person in the piano
transforms to her/his own piano
and walks piano-style to an audience member...
"Play your favorite tune"
suggests the piano.
The piano boop-beeps a few notes
until the audience member finds the magic key
(it's perfectly within union rules
to give out a few clues here.)
Once the magic key is hit
(and let's face it even if it isn't)
the piano player gets a kiss.

f. slot machine

The slot machine and players
each transform to slot machines.
With lever arms raised
and fun machine voices
they jog-jag out to the audience and ask:

"Would you like to play my slot machine?
Put a coin in my mouth
and pull my lever."

Then the audience member pulls the lever
and the slot machine sounds off
as if apples and cherries are registering.
The 5 lemons come up in a row!
and the audience member gets a jackpot kiss.

(It's better than money
lasts longer
is more honest
and is not subject to inflation or depression.)

g. strength tester

The bell sets up on stage.
A player takes an imaginary mallet
and goes to the audience member to ask
"Come up on stage and test your strength."
When s/he comes up
give him/her the imaginary mallet.
Direct him/her where to hit (if help is needed).
The player will soon discern
that the softer
      more human
      less competitive the swing is
the more the bell will respond.
Until
with the tiniest touch
the barometer goes way up to the top
and the bell stands up
and gives the player a kiss.
(It's more fun and more ecological
than a teddy bear.)

After the games have gone on long enough
(you can tell)
one actor sounds a whistle

AND

14. The Sports Events

begin.
Each sporting event is played with proper spirit
but at the climactic moment
the players give up their competition
and give a kiss.

a. a wrestling ring is formed.
   2 trainers give their women wrestlers
   last minute instructions.
   A referee introduces the wrestlers.
   They shake hands.
   A bell rings.
   The fight begins.
   The women circle one another
   grunting
   threatening.
   After 3 falls
   they head furiously for one another
   and KISS!

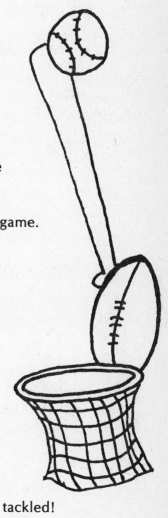

b. the men form a baseball game.
   All the players dance a cool rock dance
   as they throw the ball around
   getting ready to play.
   The umpire announces the start of the game.
   The pitcher throws a ball
   a strike and
   another ball
   (after each, he and the rest of the cast
   dance out their happiness or dismay).
   Then the batter gets a hold of one and
   bats a home run.
   As he rounds the bases
   he KISSES the base men!

c. in a football game
   2 teams huddle and then line up.
   As soon as the ball is snapped
   the players go into slow motion
   and the player who has caught the ball
   throws kisses to the audience as s/he is tackled!

d. a basketball game
   is played in a high stepping style.

A player dribbles the ball down the court.
One team makes a basket
and 2 players both take hold of the rebound
(2 players from opposite teams)
and the ref motions for a jump ball.
The 2 line up
but as the whistle is blown
they forget about the ball
and kiss each other!

e. In a slow motion boxing match
   one player is beaten to the ground
   and as the referee is counting to 10
   over the fallen person
   the other feels so bad s/he begins to cry.
   S/he pushes the ref away
   and kisses the opponent!

f. 2 lines of karate opponents face each other
   and advance in a fierce stylized manner.
   They meet
   and KISS!

After the sports events
comes the final
best of all game:

15. Kiss Relay

The actors form 2 lines
and compete with each other to see
which line can pass a kiss down the line
and back
the fastest.

            They kiss on the elbow
                        hair
                        hand.
              Then they turn to the
                    audience and say

"It's your turn!"
The players quickly divide the audience into 2 teams.
The audience gets ready
                              set
then they go!

Each audience team member
passes the kiss from one to the other
as the cast cheers them on.
(Cheer the shy ones extra hard when they hesitate.)
The audience team
then passes its kiss to the end that
most quickly wins.
But of course everyone wins!

And the show ends

and something else

BEGINS

as people who came into the theatre

as strangers

go as communal celebrants.

(

6

YOUNG PEOPLE'S THEATRE OF CELEBRATION

Let the schools of this land
be filled with a fervent
        fun
        expressive
        entertaining and
        educating theatre of celebration.
Can it be done?
Nothing, absolutely nothing, would be easier.
Schools are the greatest untapped source of theatre in the nation—
starting in kindergarten and ending in that far side of paradise called
graduate school.

     Paradoxical as it may first appear, the reason school is the exact,
right place for the theatre event in this country is that it is part of a
system:

this means it has rooms usually tidy
               probably drab
               always cold or overheated
but whatever the condition, it has available, useable space.
Furthermore, each system provides a tight, enclosed society which the
theatre event can mirror and speak to, which it can celebrate. All of us

who are there or who have been there know that:
each school in this land has its special touch
feel
its special people
power
processes
each school understands certain jokes
punches and problems
comedies and tragedies
that no other body of people in the world
can understand quite so completely.
And each school has people-power. Wow, does it have people-power!
In the schools today there are legions of young people.
They are restless
> bored
> creative
> hip.

They are ready.
There is such a fund of human energy in the schools, so vast
so promising
so wasted
which could be put to good use in the theatre,
that the mind does flip-flops at the very thought of it.

Now the professional establishment theatre is not unaware of the school's potential for theatre. What it is most aware of is what most serves its economic needs: namely it is abundantly aware that the school's young people provide ready, ofttimes captive, audiences. "Thar's box office gold in them thar educatin' pot hills. What's more thar's foundation support if you perform thar." So every spring or so, regular as crab grass, some establishment theatre somewhere trots out a *Macbeth,* puts in its farm team of actors and sends it out on a high cultural mission to the schools. Just as *Silas Marner* tells the schools how removed from their experience literature is, *Macbeth* leads them to a similar non-appreciation of theatre.

This is not to say that every touring production of *MacBeth* or Mac-what-have-you is a vast bore to young people, but too many of them are for us to rest easy about it. Equally dangerous, most touring productions teach the young people over and over again exactly what they do not need to learn. Ever! Most productions teach them that theatre is something only others can do—never the young people themselves. All the young can do is to

pay the admission price when they go in

try to keep from talking or otherwise participating while they're there

eagerly await the inevitable, if somewhat long in coming, finale.

But wait a minute, there is theatre in the schools other than touring productions. What about the theatre that the young people do themselves? Every year there's a junior class play, a senior class play and a play from any other class that's allowed to get it up to put it on. Well, to return to the question, what about it? Some are fine, but too many are not. Not because of the quality of the *production*. Due to the energy, talent, and indomitable spirit of the young people involved, the productions themselves usually zoom and swing. What is inadmissible is the *quality* of the material. Usually (not always, but *usually*) the plays are either so removed from the lived experience of the young people that they are lamentable or so inane that they are laughable(not laugh-with-able but laugh-at-able). Then, to add insult to injury, from among the legions of talented people (and they are all talented, *all of them*) only the select few are chosen. These are usually the same few who are chosen for everything else. The rest wait in the wings—as if to practice for their subservient role later on, after school is over, and the real thing has begun.

Now this elite comedy of errors must stop and the vitally necessary, the inevitable, must happen. The young people must be allowed to do material from their own lives that reveals themselves, their solitary selves and their public selves. They must be allowed to do a theatre which deals with and celebrates their passion, their identity, their person in all aspects—and not their person as seen through the commmercial camera of Hollywood, or the reactionary eye of Broadway, or the inane selections of Baker and French. It's their

person as *seen* by themselves
  as *created* by themselves
  as *performed* by themselves that's needed.

Again, wait a minute. All these young people are not equally talented and trained performers. How dare they do a play in public? It's easy. It's ever so easy. All acting really takes is a quality called mimesis. No matter how fancy the word sounds, everyone's got it. And everyone *does* it, some better at first than others, but everyone does it.

What is mimesis? It is the imitating of another's behavior, speech, idiosyncracies. This imitating is so instinctive that it's hard not to do it. Watch people at a movie get expressions of terror on their faces when one of the screen images is in danger. That's mimesis. Ultimately, taken a bit further and with a little educating experience and a lot of freedom, that's acting.

It's true that mimesis, like a lot of our natural, instinctive responses has been dulled by years of "education" but we can revive it. All it takes is will and practice. The young people have the will. Let them have the practice: let them act
     write
     create and
     do theatre
   each and every part of it
   each and every one of them.
Let them practice the theatre so they can get to know it in a way that only those who *do* something can know it.

Young people should not be the passive slugs that television forces them to be. They should be the active creators which their own natures want them to be. So let them have a theatre where they can create to their own energetic content. Some of the young creators who come out of such a theatre experience may go on and on, creating more and more sophisticated and universal works. Others may just get the pleasure of creating their own theatre and then transfer that pleasure in creating to other work. No one knows till s/he tries. And to that degree our public school system prevents so many from trying, to that same degree do they prevent so many from knowing. This vicious, ignorant circle must be stopped, dead on, before the public school system of this nation dares use the word "educate" to describe what they do and get paid for doing.

Now granted it is necessary for the young people to make their own theatre out of and with themselves, *how* do they do it? As with most everything else in this world, there are hundreds of ways. Here's a way that some young people did it. Because both the process and the results were satisfying for them and for the audience, let me detail the procedure for you. Then, should you wish

you can do something similar
(or maybe you already have)
or you can modify it to your active imagination's content
or you can go in a totally different direction.
However you may want to use the experience, here it is.

I asked a class of young people to recreate an experience from their own lives. Of that experience I asked only that it be sufficiently vital to have affected them deeply.

No matter how long ago it may have happened, the experience must still be part of them, still living, still lurking, just below the surface of their everyday consciousness.

After the class had decided on a personal memory, this charge was to plug into its current until they were recharged with its force. Once at full voltage, they were to relive the experience, first for themselves and finally, once they were ready, for an audience.

They were to relive the experience as their memory permitted
not adding frills
not adding anything.
The assumption was that just as their personal experience had been sufficiently interesting to occupy and preocupy them, so it would be interesting for others. After all, a divisive culture not withstanding, we are not so very much different one from another. What vitally interests one living person will, in all likelihood, interest another.

That was the general philosophy of the event. The practical directions
given each actor-creator were as follows:

*1. Sift through personal experience until you come up with
something you want to re-experience yourself and share with
others.*

*2. Recall and write down your personal experience in as exact
detail as possible.*

Remember the time of day
   the furniture, if inside
   the landscape, if outside.
Remember the other people involved
     what they said
     how they stood
     how they sounded
     what they wore.
Remember what you wore
     what you wanted from that experience
     what you got.
Remember anything and everything you can.
Imagine you are an artist painting the event
or better yet a photographer snapping its picture.
Get it all down
every detail.
No matter how seemingly insignificant
the details may seem to you now,
taken all in all
they will help the event to live for you.

*3. If your experience involved more people than you alone,
you can select others from your class to portray whoever is
needed.*

4. Then, together, you should assemble any properties
          clothing
          furniture
          scenic elements

you need to create your story and
                    project your story to the audience.
Use your imagination:
a scarf can be butterfly wings
a person walking on a table looks like a giant if someone is
beside him/her on the floor.
Two or three orange crates can be a bed
                              table
                              chair
                              boat
                              prison cell
                              hell.

Anything can be anything.
It's all up to you.

*5. Once you have the nuts and bolts in place for your
character and your scene get your group together and start to
improvise the event.*
Improvise it again and again
till you get it to the state
                    form and
                    content that you want.

6. Now rehearse your scene.
Rehearse it again, until you are sure it's up to snuff and ready
to go.

7. Now share it with your audience.

If all this sounds simple, it's because it is. The fact that in this
young people's theatre of celebration the actor has to be everything—
writer, director, scene designer, and properties person—is just fine. It
is a great antidote to the fragmentation of modern education which
produces so many specialists that no one can blow her/his nose
without one specialist to pass on the correct use of the handkerchief
and another to measure the wind velocity proceeding from the acti-
vated nostrils.

Granted some of the young people who are doing everything in this theatre may decide later in life that scene design or directing is the most interesting to them because they don't much want to write or direct or act any more. *But they will never know until they've tried it all.*

Further, whatever they finally decide to do in the theatre (or out of it) they will make a better choice after having done all its component parts. Actively seeing a thing through from beginning to end is of inestimable value. I don't mean seeing it through the way some schools ask you to do it, either. For example, when, in a production, young people are put on a stage crew and told to "hammer *these* nails in *that* board" and are never asked their opinion and are never allowed to do anything else, then they are not really learning about stage construction or design or anything else. It is not that hammering a nail *per se* is worthless. Far from it. It all depends on the way it's treated. If the hammering is allowed to be a respected part of the whole process which the hammerers can *understand,* then it's genuinely educational. But if it's fragmented, if the hammerers or the actors or the ticket takers or whoever are not allowed to understand their part in the whole process, then they learn nothing of real value. Then they are like the people on the assembly line at General Motors who put the wheels on a car and tighten them up. Never are they permitted by management to learn anything about the car's motor. They are only given a simple job which anyone else can do and which requires no decision-making and no creativity. They don't feel essential to the task of putting the car together because they aren't essential. They could be fired and other workers hired with little trouble to management. The workers know this and that knowledge of their expendibility helps management "keep them in their place."

In the same way, if young people are never allowed to learn the why and wherefore of their theatre task, they can be kept in their place by an elite management in theatre. Just remember education—all education—should liberate not enslave
should broaden not narrow
should release not enclose
should share not exclude
should serve not exploit.

It was to this liberating, broadening service that the young people in my class came up with experiences from their own life and shared them with an audience. The scenes ranged from tragic to comic; from events involving one person to events involving ten; from realistic to surrealistic; and from everyday experiences to daydreams and night dreams.

Here's a sampling:

A young, gangling, nervous girl, physically uncoordinated, of 15 years tries out for cheerleading.

A young man of 16 is at the casket of his close friend, a friend who had been with him for years—stealing bicycles, turning on, doing the things poor, restless, desperate young inner-city people do. Now the young best friend is dead.

A young girl of 3 years wants, demands, screams for chocolate pudding for dessert. No matter how much her parents offer lemon pie, she continues her yelping, tearful demands. She eventually gets her dessert, not the pudding, but the lemon pie—right in her 3-year-old face.

A young man of 16 finds out, in one crushing moment, that his girl friend has just died of sickle-cell anemia.

Two young girls of 8 play their talk game of adding "o" to every word they say. "Theyo-refuseo-too-giveo-upo-theiro-gameo" even when they are being questioned by the school principal.

A young man of 15 plays roughhouse with towels in a locker room until, suddenly, inexplicably and embarrassedly he becomes sexually aroused.

A young person of 6 gets lost on her way home from school and is afraid to ask directions because her parents schooled her not to talk to strangers.

A young woman of 15 is at a dance and extraordinarily proud of the fact that she is now "of an age" to be wearing her first brassiere.

A young man of 16 gives the pep talk of his life to his team mates who are about to play a football rival, only to return, post-game, suffering the defeat of his life.

A young woman dreams. In her dream, there is a strange knocking at the door. Her mother tries to keep the door closed but a man dressed as a woman forces his way into the house and picks up the mother and carries her off.

Two young people of 8 are playing spaceship. As they are reeling through space, bouncing off one planet then another, the young boy hears a thud. His dog has been hit by a car. No one is home. He tries to call an ambulance. No one will come. They will only come for people. They refuse to understand that his dog is a person.

A young man tearfully discovers during a talk with a close friend that the close friend is a homosexual.

A young man of 14 comes home to find his father drunk and desperately needing a release from his loneliness. The father's way of reaching out is to find fault with whatever his son does. Neither one says to the other what they really need from one another, but it is clear that they both know what they need, and it is equally clear that they never express it.

A young girl of 7 goes to her dying grandmother's bedside to reassure her beloved grandparent that everything will be all right: that she will get well and come home soon. She is not to worry. When her grandparent gets home they can go on with their cha-cha lessons and she can watch the Lawrence Welk show on T.V. all she wants; there will be no more arguments. "Only just come home," the young girl says to her grandmother, "I love you so much."

There were more scenes, many more. What evolved from all of them was *theatre*—a theatre woven from the fabric and the fiber of the lives of the young people who created it. The results were tremblingly honest, they were funny, they were sad, they were heartbreaking, they were hilarious. The scenes touched everyone who saw them in the way theatre is meant to but seldom does. For, in this theatre, actors were not showing off, not proving how "professionally" they could do a piece of convention. No. Here were young people honestly reliving those intensely personal moments which they carry about with them and which color the rest of their lives.

What both the actors and the audience discovered at this people's theatre was that these experiences, while personal, were not exclusive.

Everyone said, over and over again, "that was me," "I had an experience just like that," or "that was what my childhood was like." So in the midst of these essentially personal, solitary experiences a solidarity was discovered. Theatre can do no more than this: to forge, to affirm a living link between us all.

We performed this people's theatre for high schoolers, for college people, and at homes for the long-living. While all these audiences were fun and had fun, the audience of the long-living was an especially fulfilling experience. How rewarding to see long-living people of 70 or 80 or 90 smilingly recall their own lives as they watched their younger counterparts. A life cycle was formed here, a continuum binding one age to the other.

> "We are not so different after all,"
> one long-living man of around 80 said.
> "Not so different."

AN AFTERWORD: THEATRE IN HOMES FOR THE LONG-LIVING

Two young students who did personal-experience people's theatre with me in a workshop, adapted the idea to their own interest: doing theatre for and with the long-living. The women, Susan Bruyn and Robin Smith, went to the Washington Manor Housing Project in South Boston and set up an in-house people's theatre. It would be worthwhile to share their procedure and experience with you in case you want to do something similar.

In the beginning Robin and Susan spent a good deal of time
getting to know the people in the project (age range 60-90).
After their mutual introduction to each other and
the establishment of a bond of trust
they invited the people to tell stories about themselves.
Everyone (Robin and Susan included) told personal-life
stories for a couple of weeks.
Then Robin and Susan structured the experience a bit more:
they asked the people
to tell stories related to a theme: a school day
first love
mischief.

EXAMPLE: THE SCHOOL DAY

Myra remembered she had been late to school.

Mabel remembered she had fought a lot in school.

Francisco remembered that he loved going to school.

Isabel remembered that she tried to be teacher's pet.

Robin and Susan then developed improvisations around these themes. The improvisation was so designed that each person could use elements of his/her memory to help create a theatre piece in which everyone interacted with everyone else.

EXAMPLE: THE SCHOOL DAY IMPROVISATION

Robin played the teacher

Myra played the class clown, always cutting up and getting people to laugh.

Mabel tried to pick fights with Francisco (because she wanted him to notice her).

Francisco tried to avoid both the clowning Myra and the fighting Isabel in a rather futile attempt to listen to the teacher.

Isabel actively tried to stop the clowning and fighting (to prove to the teacher how much she liked her and, in turn, deserved to be liked herself).

The improvisation proved both fun and instructive. Myra summed it up this way: "We learn new things about ourselves from past experiences."

Another part of Robin's and Susan's experience was equally as valuable for us as the procedure for the improvisation and the success of it: the young women discovered that not all the long-living people wanted to join the improvisation or even the storytelling. Some were too shy.

At first Robin and Susan were disappointed, thinking they had failed in some way. But they soon learned to take heart from the fact that the long-living people ventured out of their rooms and came together to be together whereas in the past they had lived shut off from each other, each one feeling that no one else really wanted his/her company.

What was discovered here was that people coming together to be with people is good people's theatre. IT'S REAL GOOD PEOPLE'S THEATRE.

THEATRE IN A FACTORY

I have used the same storytelling in creating theatre in a factory. I was invited to a factory in Saugus, Massachusetts to do theatre with a group of workers, many of whom had not been in a theatre since they were kids—if then.

First we played tag with a time card.
Then we did an improvisation:
I divided the group in two. I told each group a secret which was to influence their action toward the other group (but which they were not to divulge to the other group).
I told group A that they were the workers in the factory and were to try a new tack with management in order to get management to understand their needs: they were to invite management to their homes that evening and, over dinner, have along discussion about their worker-needs. No matter what management did to offend them, they were not to act offended—the important thing was to get management to their homes.
I told group B that they were management at the factory. They were to offend the workers in order to get the workers to quit the plant so the workers would not be entitled to a new retirement plan that would cost management more than they wanted to pay. If the workers were fired, management would have to pay the retirement; if the workers quit, the management did not have to pay.
The conditions of the improvisation understood, the groups of people interacted with each other for around a half hour.
It was a rewarding
       instructional
       group unifying good time.
Then we sat down, had lunch, and told stories about ourselves, most of which were related to the working conditions at the plant.
After lunch and storytelling, we divided in groups of two to four and acted out the stories.
To understand the powerful human force of that experience you needed to be there. But, of course, you can engender the

same force.
Go to a factory
       housing development
       prison
       wherever there are people who need to experience
       their own passion in their own theatre.

Build trust
Unite the group
Invite them to tell their own stories
and then act out the stories.
Remember, acting out personal stories
is a custom just about as old as the life of the human race.
So there's nothing magical about *how* to do it.
There's just something magical in seeing it done and
                         in doing it.
So get with it.
Create some people-magic.

Susan Bruyn and Robin Smith at the Washington Manor Housing Project in South Boston.

7

MAYAN
THEATRE
A QUEST MADE
AND AN HOMAGE PAID

We have been talking about people's theatre of celebration:

> scenarios for it
> how to do it
> where to do it
> who can do it
> when to do it
> why to do it.

Before discussing more kinds of people's theatres, it would be worthwhile to ask ourselves if this populist idea in American theatre is something new: did it spring full-blown the other day or has it been around for a long time? The answer, as you might guess, is that it's been around for a time. What you might not guess is just how long that time is. People's theatre in the Americas began long before our present numbering centuries began: it flourished not only pre-Columbian but pre-Christ. It is to that ancient source that we will now look for our justification and inspiration.

QUESTION: Establishment theatres are wont to trace their heritage from the Greeks and Romans to the Middle Ages in England and then to find a full flowering in the Western European Renaissance. Isn't that where those of us in people's theatre should look for our heritage?

ANSWER: Quite the reverse. It is absolutely necessary that we reach back beyond colonialist-imposed culture to find our roots. In *The Wretched of the Earth,* Franz Fannon explains why:

> The passion to search for a national culture which existed before the colonial era finds its legitimate reason in the anxiety shared by the native intellectuals to shrink away from that Western culture in which they all risk being swamped.... And let us make no mistake, it is with the greatest delight that they discover that there is nothing to be ashamed of in the past but rather dignity, glory, and solemnity. The claim to a national culture in the past rehabilitates that nation and serves as a justification for the hope of a future culture. [1]

The pre-colonial culture from which we will now get our hope is that of the ancient Maya. This extraordinary Indian culture—described as the Hellenic culture of the Americas—flourished in Central America from two to three centuries before Christ until the sixteenth century when invading Spaniards purposefully decimated them. And it had, as nearly as I can judge, one of the first or the very first recorded theatre of the Americas.[2]

Although, as we have said, the invading Spaniards did all they could to destroy this civilization, they did not succeed. Due to the tenacity and ingenuity of the Maya, enough has survived about them and through them to yield the following information:

> Their diet was infinitely superior to that of contemporary Europeans.
> Their wells for water storage and their road systems rivaled those of Rome.
> By critical consensus their polychromatic pottery was as good as that of the Greeks.

They developed the concept of zero before it was known in
North Africa or Europe.
Their pyramids were as broad, as high, as magnificent, and
have proved to be as long-lived as those of the Egyptians.
These "primitive" Americans, moreover, developed a system
of hieroglyphic writing, correctly counting the "steps to the
moon," and designing a calender more accurate than our
own.
They formulated philosophical ideas about the nature of
man and the universe that were strikingly modern in
complexity and cynicism.
They were seafaring, unwarlike, and greatly artistic.

It is not only the quality but the sheer quantity of Mayan art that
is amazing. It is but a slight exaggeration to say that their art
permeated every part of their daily life. Weaving, marketing, wall
design, clothing, pottery making, religion and architecture—all were
interpenetrate with art. People, then, did not—like their "civilized"
counterparts today—leave off the one to take up the other. For these
"primitives" to pray
to cook
to market
to live at all
was to be engaged in art.[3]

If we went no further in our investigation of the Mayan than to
note the fact that this greatly human civilization did not separate their
art from their life; that instead, they used their art to enhance the daily
lives of their people, we in the people's theatre could walk away with
incomparable justification for what we are about and with incomparable hope for the future. Fully applying this single concept, we
could revitalize theatre—and all art—in this country.

The practical implications
of art and life being interpenetrate mean that
art need not be only on special occasions
with special people
for special people

in special places
it means that art is a *part of people's lives*, not divorced from them.

QUESTION: How exactly did theatre's being a part of life work?
ANSWER: It worked in such a way that in the daily life of the Mayan, theatre became an absolute necessity. Here's how their theatre-generating dynamic went:

The Maya had gods for almost every activity of daily life and
it was absolutely necessary to celebrate and
                                    placate these gods
so the gods would help Mayan life to run as smoothly as possible. Therefore, festivals were dedicated to the gods, entire months were devoted to each festival and
                    with few exceptions
each festival had dance-theatre especially designed for it.
The dance-theatre was, at one and the same time, useful to placate the gods and
to benefit daily life and
to please the people.

Like most people's theatres since, the Mayan dance-theatre was accompanied by music and it was greatly enlivened by audience participation. Never ones to sit quietly back, these ancient Indians entered into their dance-theatre experience with handclapping, cries, and stamping. Some dances, to be sure, were performed by skilled dancers but others, the entire community danced.[4] It has been estimated that thousands of Indians would come from miles around to perform their dance-theatre of life.

Existing side by side with this ritualistic dance-theatre was a theatre which, although using music, dance, and mask, relied more heavily on words. These "complete plays", like the other kinds of Mayan theatre, were performed in the open air, in the atria or plazas of temples. Having as their permanent setting the surrounding jungle, they—like the dance theatre—pulsated with sound, both natural and human made. In the heirarchy of Mayan theatre, the spoken dramas seem to have occupied a select place since they were reserved for very important occasions:

the most important festival months
the celebration of the New Year and its calendar
divisions
the consecration of the idols during the month
of Mol
the sacred ball games.

We know very little about the plays which the ancient Maya performed. As we have noted, the conquering Spaniards—like the conquerors of Native Americans in North America—were loathe to preserve anything which gave the Indians a sense of community and identity. So the Spaniards destroyed virtually all Mayan plays. We do know from chroniclers that the Mayan drama repertoire, like the dance repertoire, was very large. Furthermore, we know from the one play that managed to survive something of their drama's form, content, and reason for being.

The extant Mayan word play is best known by the name of its noble protagonist, *Rabinal*. It is based on a long and legendary battle between the Mayan tribes of Quiche and Rabinal. When the play begins, the proud leader of the Maya-Quiche, Quiche-Achi, has been captured by Rabinal. Quiche-Achi is tried and condemned to death but before his sentence is carried out, he is permitted, because of the complete confidence the Mayan's had in one another's word, to return "to his people, to his valleys, and to his mountains." At the end of the reprieve granted him, fixed at "thirteen times twenty days and thirteen times twenty nights," he returns to the court of Rabinal and, inexorably, his sentence is carried out.[5] What this analysis of the play reveals is that:

Rabinal is not a play for the sake of religion: there is no mention of the gods and the priests appear only to dress the stage.
Rabinal is not a history play: the precise historical moment of the play is never even defined.
Rabinal is simply a play that: transports the actors and audience to an imaginary place and asks them to exalt in the real qualities of the Mayan people: qualities that the Mayan

people themselves most prize; a spirit of gentleness and
courage and honesty.

Rabinal is, in a word, people's theatre.

I would like to conclude this all-too-brief section on Native
American people's theatre with a roll call of some present day Indian
theatres. The continuity between past and present will be most
obvious, as will its application for the future of the people's theatre
movement in this country.

CIRCLE FILM INC.
A NATIVE AMERICAN STORYTELLER'S ASSOCIATION:

> We live, work, present our stories from within the great circle
> of our days on Mother Earth. We have been given stories to
> tell to our brothers and sisters. We have gifts to give. We
> know that in the circle of our lives, the gifts go out, rise into
> the air of America like smoke of a soft wind, hang in the
> thoughts and dreams of the people and return to the earth
> where we are, someday. There is always a great hunger
> among people for stories. If we can make these subtle and
> exciting, complex and powerful, simple and clear tales rise
> into the air through our humble actions, then we believe this
> is an addition to the health of all the people, however far
> from direct and natural the media used may seem.

(For a copy of CIRCLE FILM's statements about
themselves and further information write them: P.O. Box
2900, Santa Fe, New Mexico 87501)

NATIVE AMERICAN PERFORMING ARTISTS:

> They perform music/dance/song pieces which they create
> together out of the rich lore of Native Americans.

(Write them at: 2543 Harriet Avenue, Minneapolis, MN.
55405)

RED EARTH PERFORMING ARTS COMPANY

> Located in Seattle they began in mid-1974 and are currently
> attempting to build a repertoire of Indian written plays with
> composition, directing, and acting by an all-Indian theatre

company. They have built their repertoire to almost a dozen pieces and have done some touring. Two pieces which they have toured recently are *Changer*, which dramatizes the Skokomish tradition of the creation of the world, and *Raven*, based on a story in Northwest Coast mythology.

(Write them at: 3602 West Government Way Extension, Seattle WA 98199)

SPIDERWOMAN THEATRE WORKSHOP

They create theatre/poetry/music pieces for and with the Indian community in New York. One such event was created in the Fall of 1975 as a benefit for Yvonne Wanrow and was very successful in bringing together varied people in New York to work towards a sense of identity and cultural pride.

(Write Muriel Miguel, 333 De Graw Street, Brooklyn, N.Y.)

NAVAJO TRUCKING COMPANY

They were instrumental in creating an Indian company which has performed several plays on the reservation including performances for a meeting of national Indian health workers and officials.

(Write Grace Clashin, Navajo Community College, Tsaile, Arizona 86556)

LAS CUCARACHAS

They present programs of Chicana art, poetry, theatre, music, and dance—including images of Indian women.

(Contact Dorinda Moreno and Cocilio Mujeres, 725 Rhode Island, San Francisco, CA 94107)

WHITE ROOTS OF PEACE

They are creating a theatre piece dealing with the Wounded Knee occupation.

(contact *Akwesasne Notes*)

NATIVE AMERICAN MEDIA PROGRAM

This group maintains that no minority has suffered so much in the loss of their self-image through the influence of television as the American Indian through the Western portrayals of savages or ridiculous caricatures. The group is monitoring and assessing television programming, is developing contact with key people in the television industry, sharing information and assessments with media people, assisting Indian groups in getting media visibility, developing connections with other media-oriented groups (especially in minority communities), and publishing newsletters of its findings and activities.

(Write Stella Montoaya, 980 North Fair Oaks Avenue, Pasadena, CA 91103)

All the above information came from a newsletter printed by a leader of the people's cultural network, Ms. Linda Walsh Jenkins (a former student of mine who is teaching me what it is essential that I learn about current Indian theatre). To share with you the soul and commitment of the people who make up the people's movement, let me quote Ms. Jenkins describing her role in researching and promoting Native American theatre.

I work as an active facilitator of the development and spread of contemporary Native American performance as well as working as a researcher into the Native performance life of this continent. As a facilitator I have established a communications network among Indian performing artists, educators, and journalists in North America. This network produces an annual newsletter for several hundred Indian and non-Indian people, and the newsletter is supplemented with one-page bulletins sent occasionally to the producing Indian theatre companies in the United States. In this way, we can pass along information regarding grants, new plays, jobs, training programs, tour or residency problems, etc.

As a researcher and historian I seek to formulate questions about creative energies of the past which might serve to illuminate our paths today. I am working on a study of the performance of visions in Native North America which will yield a casebook; this may offer heuristic models and inspiration for those of us who recognize the need for holistic theatre/community events today. I am also working with Ed Wapp, jr. (Commanche/Sac and Fox) on a study of the pow-wow, a twentieth century Indian performance event with roots in traditional performance; this offers insight into twentieth century Indian ways. I will not publish anything on Indian performance without approval, encouragement, and preferably collaboration with Indian friends. I will not take money for myself for the sale of anything I publish unless it is money I can turn back into the newsletter and the transcontinental phone calls that involves. I believe every non-Indian attempting to write about Indian people should do the same.

There is a spirit in this land which was nurtured by the Native American people over thousands of years. The prophets of these people have challenged us all to heed this spirit. We have obligations to that spirit and those prophets, for the sake of our own spirit and for what we might become.[6]

FOOTNOTES

1. Franz Fannon, *The Wretched of the Earth,* Grove Press, New York, 1966, p. 210.
2. Lisa Paret Limardo, *La Danda del Venado en Guatemala,* Guatemala, 1964, p.10. Other books I have consulted are: S.G. Morely's, *The Ancient Maya,* London, 1946; J.E.S. Thompson's, *The Rise and Fall of the Mayan Civilization, Oklahoma, 1966; Pefro Henriques Utena's, A Concise History of Latin American Culture,* trans. Gilbert Chase, New York, 1947.
I also spent the better part of three years in Guatemala, experiencing first-hand the ruins and remnants of that extraordinary American culture.
3. To be sure, many other Native American cultures subsequent to the Maya (and maybe some prior to them) have had glorious people's cultures. And all these indigenous cultures deserve not only passing mention but intensive study. Since, however, this is primarily an idea and practical book, not a history, this is not the time or space to undertake that investigation. The reason we will take time out for this all-too-brief look at the pre-colonial Mayan culture is to signal the need for such studies.
4. The Maya had many centers devoted exclusively to training performers.
5. Marcial Armas Lara, *El Renacimineto de la Danu Guatemalteca,* Sociedad de Geografia e Historia de Guatemala, Guatemala, 1964, p.44-67
6. A personal letter sent to me by Ms. Linda Jenkins.

8

NEWSTHEATRE

Whoever said that theatre has to be a fiction created by an established playwright?

theatre has to last two to four hours?

theatre must cost a lot of money for those who do it and for those who watch it?

theatre has to follow a conventional plot with conventional characters who end up, in one way or another, supporting the conventional order?

theatre has to take place in a formal stage setting with seats in rows facing it?

theatre has to be divorced from the political and economic needs of the day?

theatre cannot educate the people?

theatre cannot serve the people?

Whoever told colleges that what happened in the 17th century is of more theatrical worth than what is happening today?

Whoever told "serious" actors that they must prove their worth by acting Hamlet or Lady MacBeth?

Whoever told Broadway and off-Broadway and off-off-Broadway that sex was the only "commodity" that really interests an audience?

Whoever told New York and Hollywood that a person with principles to the left of the established order eventually forsakes her/his principles and joins the established order:

i.e.

Idealist:	I told you I can't do it
Big Shot:	For $10,000?
Idealist:	I told you, no!
Big Shot:	For $20,000?
Idealist:	I'll do it.

i.e.

Pacifist:	I could never kill a human being.
Realist:	That man just raped your wife!
Pacifist:	I'll kill him!

i.e.

Resisting Woman:	You must go home, John. I've got to get back to work. The first draft of my book must be on the publisher's desk tomorrow.
He Man:	(Grabs her and kisses her. Hard. Long.)
Resisting Woman:	(Appropriately panting) Oh John! (Another kiss. More appropriate panting.) Oh John, John, John!
He Man:	(Starts to leave.)
Resisting Woman:	(Alarmed) Where are you going?

He-man: (His eyes wander up and
                                       down her quivering body)
                                       Home ... don't you have to get
                                       back to your book?
Resisting Woman: (Tearing up her manuscript.)
                                       What book?

Whoever told everyone in establishment theatre that the only
           audiences who have "taste" live in New York City
           followed—but not too closely—by a few "select"
           audiences of refinement in a few other "select"
           metropolitan areas?

Whoever told the makers of theatre that

           fat women are either slovenly or funny?

           black men are either criminal or sexy?

           diamonds—and husbands or lovers who give
           them—are a girl's best friend?

           people without a lot of money are of *less* intrinsic
           and extrinsic worth than people with a lot of
           money?

Whoever told the makers of theatre that

           put down jokes about age or sex are funny?

           beautiful women and working class people are
           either animalistically shrewd or just plain dumb?

           intelligent women are dry as a birch weed in
           autumn?

Whoever said white men, rulers, kings, celebrities, and the "beautiful
           people" are the subjects of theatre?

           minorities, women and the economically disad-
           vantaged are the objects for those subjects?

Who knows who said these things, as absurd as they are cruel? One thing we do know is that ideas like these have long influenced the subject and form of establishment theatre in this country. Whoever the people were who initiated such ideas, *they were wrong!*

People are beginning to be aware that

> theatre need not be about a "select" few heroes and kings; it can be about those people who are most of the people on the land.

> theatre need not be a tool of wealth and power; it can be a voice speaking to and about the people.

> theatre need not be a commodity dictated by what sells and sells out;
> it can be dictated by the needs of the people.

> theatre need not be barbarous, crude, and sensational;
> it can be a force engaging and enlarging the people's conscience, vision, and sense of self-worth.

> theatre need not be out of the past and romantic; it can be immediate and to the point.

People are beginning to be aware that theatre can address itself to something other than

> *Hamlet, Camelot* (and all the rest of the kings, queens and heir-apparents who wonder "what the simple folk do?")

> *The Rothschilds (Philadelphia Story, Way of the World,* and *Private Lives* of the elegant, rich, and controlling 2%)

> *Funny Lady,* Winston Churchill, FDR, Lenny Bruce, *Mack and Mabel* (and all the rest of the super stars).

Any Wednesday, School for Wives, (and all the
rest of the lovely, young virginal types).

Gingerbread Lady, Mrs. Malaprop, *Streetcar
Named Desire* (and all the rest of the silly
or neurotic—what else?—women over
40).

In sum, people are beginning to be aware that contra-people
theatre has been going on for too long a time. So it's high time for
another kind of for-the-people theatre.

It's high time that women over 40
     Blacks
     workers
     Native Americans
     Spanish-speaking Americans
     Asian-Americans
     homosexuals
     children
     prisoners

have a fair toss of the coin in the selection and creation of events for the
theatre.

To be sure, even with a fair toss of the coin, about half the time the
dime will turn up heads and, once again, we'll get a theatre about the
high and mighty beautiful people who on stage—as off—look down
their noses at the rest of us. But, with a fair toss of the coin, about half
the time it'll turn up tails, and we can have a story about someone with
no special powers or privileges. We can have a story about someone
whose sole reason for being the subject of a theatre event would be that
s/he was a human being and that his/her humanity was of immediate,
human interest to the people.

For the fact of the matter is that all people—not just those at the
top of the heap—need to see their own lives in the theatre. Moreover,
they need to see their lives as lived, experienced, felt and desired by
themselves not as a background for, or an object of, the more
powerful. If there are no established playwrights who want to address
themselves to the lives and interests of the majority of people (or even if
there are) let the people themselves create it.

What results may not be high art, but it might be pretty good. That all depends on the time, effort, and creativity of the people involved. But whatever its artistic caliber, what will result is a theatre of, by, and for the people. And that's a concept that should be realized more often in this country—in and out of the theatre.

One sure source of immediate, humanly interesting theatre for the people is local, national, and international newspapers. Newspapers tell stories about people's festivals

> habits
> trends
> births
> deaths

> famines
> unemployment
> endurance

> needs
> losses
> loves
> meannesses
> heroism.

To be sure some newspapers may not tell the whole story. They tend to tell only what sells issues to their readers. Still, with a little ingenuity and a lot of research, we can fill in the lines between the lines and come up with a people's newstheatre.
Here's how to do it.

Get together a group of committed people, say 6 to 60 (read those numbers as applying to quantities and ages of the people). *Scour the papers and magazines for a story that interests you and/or is relevant to the interests and needs of your community.* (Remember to keep your eye cocked for those stories that ought to make the papers but don't.) For example, in one newstheatre which I supervised, an actor/writer/director/designer person named James Simpson turned into theatre a story about two men who took a raft out into the Atlantic Ocean. This is the reason Mr. Simpson gave for choosing that particular newspaper incident:

"What turned me on about it? I guess it was an amalgamation of my personality and the actual news item. When I was a child, I had read *The Raft* and that had excited me. Also, I grew up in Hawaii and was fascinated and in some kind of awe about the ocean. I've had this conception about the water as man's master. I've personally never had so much fun as in the water but also never experienced such deep panic. Another thing that interested me about this story was that the two guys involved were human heroes. They weren't bad, martyrs, perverts, racists, or tainted as far as I know. Perhaps they were, but I think not. For me, anyhow, they were genuine heroes that any of us could be.

Another thing that made me want to make theatre out of them was their sense of comradery. I grew up reading tales of great friendships. My super-human heroes all had fast friendships. Alexander and Hephastion, Achilles and Patroclus. The two sea voyagers seemed to have just that, but they were real people."

Once you have the story that interests you, start the research. If people in the story are alive, you can try to meet them personally. You will, more often than not, be beautifully surprised how kind and cooperative even the busiest people prove to be. For example:

Harry Brown (White) became interested in the case of a young doctor, Kenneth Edelin (Black). Dr. Edelin had been convicted of manslaughter in Massachusetts, February of 1974, in the death of a fetus during an abortion.

Here was a story of general interest not only to Mr. Brown but to lots of people because the right of women to have control over their lives was on trial every bit as much as Dr. Edelin.

For his research, Harry Brown first read everything he could find about the trial, about abortion, and about the arguments of those for and against abortion. He then regularly attended Dr. Edelin's trial. Eventually, he succeeded not only in interviewing Dr. Edelin a number of times, but in securing his consent to come and watch the newstheatre about his case.

If people in the story are far away, you can write them or you can write the reporter who related the incident.

Here's a portion of the letter Susan Bruyn received in response to her inquiry about an IRA woman whose picture she had seen in a Hearst newspaper. The letter was written by a journalist who had reported the incident.

Dear Susan Bruyn,
No, you have not intruded. I'm delighted to help out even if it is only in a wee way. I'm interested in your fascination over Margaret McKearney so I hasten to contribute a little of addenda.

The letter (which I am not at liberty to reprint) goes on to discuss in great detail personal and political facts about the woman Margaret McKearney. All in all, it gave Ms. Bruyn more than enough data to construct an exciting piece of newstheatre.

If the locale of the story is within traveling distance (or if a similar locale is near-by) you should go there. The actors in Newstheatre which I have supervised/directed have gone to prisons

mental hospitals	zoos
police stations	factories
inner-city housing developments	racist meetings
bars	lesbian-mother meetings
inner city-schools	churches
the docks	synagogues

To be sure, calls have to be placed, strings may have to be pulled and oft-times untold requests made before permission can be secured to visit some of these places. But the effort and the waiting are more than compensated for by the experiences themselves.

Remember, you would not want anyone to enact an event from your life without first finding out as much about you as possible; neither should you enact any character, living or dead, until you have studied that person as completely as possible.

So, once you gain admittance to your locale, don't go once. Go again and again and again.

> Don't go as a tourist to say you've been.
> Go as a human being to breathe in
> > explore
> > understand
> > experience
> whatever forces in the immediate environment formed or triggered the event of your story.
> Go as an accomplice of the heart.

As you experience the environment of your character's life in your imagination you *are* the character
> this is where you live
> the people here are your friends, your enemies
> the walls here are enclosing you
> it is not another's but your own
> anguish or ecstacy
> need or excess
> that prompted you—the character—to do
> whatever you did.

Once this process of internalizing the character has started continue until you become that character.

> Begin to live an hour
> > an evening
> > a day as your character lived.
> Go to his/her haunts.
> Wear her/his rags or riches.
> Respond to his/her music.
> Move
> Feel

Act
React
in his/her rhythm.
Long his/her longings.

Once you have come to internal and external terms with the character, once you have transformed your self to her/his self, you are ready to *construct the theatre event.*

In structuring the piece, remember the facts are there to guide you. And, due to your in-depth research, you have ever so many more facts than were in the original story.

It may be, however, that when you structure the event for presentation, you will not use all the facts, *per se,* because you might decide to focus on a moment other than the one the press related. You might dramatize a day or a week before the actual event in order to show its causative circumstances.

You might dramatize a day or a year after the event to show its effects on the character and those around him/her.

You might do a continuum, dramatizing the day before, the event itself, and the moment after.

You might do two scenes: one real, showing what actually happened; one surreal, showing what the character wanted to happen or feared might happen.

Or you might do any combination or deviation of these.

Just let your imagination, passion, and compassion be your guide. Have trust in your own creativity and you will discover that countless possible ways to structure your piece will present themselves to you.

Whatever you choose to dramatize, the more your chosen event is something which excites not only your own passion, but the passion of your community at large, the more rewarding a piece of theatre you can create. Here are some examples of newstheatre which I have supervised that provoked lively community response:

A Black man in South Africa is being tortured for possessing Marxist literature.

A WAC is under investigation for demanding equality of treatment for men and women in the armed forces.

A Jehovah's Witness family refuses to let their child receive medical attention and the child dies.

Joan Little is on trial for killing the man who purportedly raped her in her cell.

An unemployed man kills his wife with an ax on the school playground while their child looks on.

A policeman comes to arrest a woman because she refused to heed a summons concerning her unleashed dog.

The press secretary of the President of the United States resigns.

A young man and a young woman enact the dating etiquette of those who attend singles bars.

A schizophrenic, driven mad by the media, proclaims that Seven-Up is the unholy drink, Coca-Cola the drink of the "goley host."

These are but examples. Every day in the papers, and in stories you hear about that ought to make the papers but don't, there are more. (And as you are creating your plays out of newspaper events remember that exciting plays like Albert Camus' *The Misunderstanding,* Athol Feugard's *Sizwi Banzi is Dead,* had their beginning in the newspapers.) *Once you have created your characters and constructed the story, rehearse it. Then rehearse it again. Then some more.*
Now put four or five newstheatre pieces together in an exciting dramatic sequence. Rehearse and rehearse and rehearse it until it is ready to be shared with an audience. And you will have theatre enough for anyone.
Now take your newstheatre to homes for the long-living
> schools
> prisons
> street corners
> wherever there are people who want to
> know and feel more about people.

How mutually beneficial it would be
if a community
  a town
  a hospital
  hosted you.

Then, every week or so, with their advice, you could dramatize events
of interest to the community.
Or you might build a theatre collective around the idea of newstheatre
          find yourself a space and
          set up shop.
Boston's Living Newspaper did precisely that.
In January, 1976, they collected some 6 people who were committed to
the struggle against oppression. Witness their statement:

> We are an open collective of actors committed to the strug-
> gles against exploitation and oppression. Newstheatre is the
> vehicle we've chosen to use in the process of transforming
> society.
> Every week we produce a brand new show that dramatizes
> current events not popularly known or accurately portrayed
> in the mass media.
> Our company, now one and a half years old, is based on the
> original "Living Newspaper" which grew out of the
> government-funded Federal Theatre during the 1930's
> Depression. We strive to demystify "the theatre," to make it
> accessible to everyone, and to encourage and help others
> form acting collectives such as ours.

They contacted sympathetic members of the people's movement;
asked for and were given space in churches and theatres in the Boston
area and they now perform at the Red Book Store and for unions,
tenants groups, strike committees, the nuclear power movement, etc.
in the area.

                    Here is a sample of their work.

GOOD NEWS FROM HAITI

information from the New York Times

One person plays the good news person. The rest of the cast sits
throughout the audience. The good news person wears a red, white,

and blue straw hat and represents the government or a corporation. Cast members in the audience represent citizens eager to *hear* the good news but quick to question what they begin to perceive is being *passed off* as good news.

(Runs onto the performing area waving a good news sign.)

Good News: Good News from your government.

(clapping enthusiastically—hopefully)

Good News: Haiti is advancing under Duvalier. The per capita income has risen in the President's five years in office.

Audience: How much has the per capita income risen?

Good News: (proudly) Since 1971, the per capita income has almost *doubled.* Not only that—the minimum wage...(hunts for figures in papers)

Audience: Excuse me. You mentioned doubling. Doubled from what to what?

Good News: What to what?

Audience: I mean figures, numbers.

Good News: (searching) Oh. (finds it) The per capita income in 1971 ranged from $60 to $75. Today it ranges from $100 to $130...per year (softly).

Audience: Per year?

SHOCKED SILENCE

Audience: What were you saying about the minimum wage?

Good News: (perking up) Oh, yes. In 1974, it increased from $1 to $1.30.

Audience: Per hour?

Good News: No...per day. (pause) But the future looks good. With helpful press coverage like this from the *New York*

Times, things are bound to get better. I quote: "Haiti offers an inexpensive and nonunionized labor force of 26,000 people, mostly women. The Haitians have a reputation for working hard. With Puerto Rico's wages approaching United States' levels and labor troubles increasing elsewhere in this region, Haiti's future as the center of the United States assembly industry appears bright...politically Haiti remains stable. Opposition...(trails off) Oh, the rest is unimportant. (starts to leave)

Audience: What about the opposition?

Good News: (reluctantly) Opposition by word or deed is BANNED. Read the *New York Times.* All the news that's print to fit. (rushes off as if to another audience) Good news, good news. Haiti advancing under Duvalier.

How beneficial to the people's network it could be if a number of people's theatres around the country created newstheatre. Just as there is a weekly newspaper, so could there be a weekly newstheatre.
The difference:

Newspapers, more often than not, are controlled by special interest groups.

Newspapers, more often than not, dwell on the surface and exploit the sensational aspects of events.

Newspapers, more often than not, pretend to an objectivity that is misleading.

But

Newstheatre will have the time and will and passion to reveal not only the surface of the story, but the stories that lie behind and give birth to the event.

Newstheatre will not pretend to an objectivity; it will tell the truth.

Newstheatre will not be on the side of commerce; it will be on the side of the people.

9
GUERRILLA THEATRE

Guerrilla theatre is people's theatre.

Guerrilla theatre arises when people perceive there is a clear and
        present danger to the community.

Guerrilla theatre arises among the impassioned.

Guerrilla theatre arises among activists who think that no matter how
        bleak the situation, there is still a chance
        to save things.

Guerrilla theatre is a call to solidarity among the few to do battle
        against a larger, more powerful force.

Guerrilla theatre is not subtle: it does not rely on complicated
        arguments to make its point. Its strength
        lies in bold
           clear
           striking images.

Guerrilla theatre —like guerrilla warfare—is always on the move.
It must be able to make its statement quickly
at any time
in any place
with little
money or
material

Then, as quickly as need be,
it must clear out
go to another place
repeat its performance.

Guerrilla theatre does not persuade the uncommitted. (It might, but the odds are against it.)

Guerrilla theatre does crystalize the situation for those already committed. It buoys them up by allowing them to celebrate the justice and solidarity (if not the immediate pragmatism) of their outcry.

Guerrilla theatre is an act of rebellion. And as Albert Camus says, rebellion is both a negative and a positive act:

"Rebellion cannot exist without the feeling that somewhere, in some way, you are justified. It is in this way that the rebel slave says yes and no at the same time. He affirms that there are limits and also that he suspects—and wishes to preserve—the existence of certain things beyond those limits." [1]

This act of bloodless rebellion
which we will call guerrilla theatre

can happen whenever there is a barricade of a building
reservation
the military

a nuclear testing protest
denial of people's rights
racism
slaughter of innocents
a civil rights march
a consumer boycott
a peace vigil
a demonstration to
support workers
women
children
prisoners
homosexuals
minority people
city people
public servants.

HERE ARE SOME WAYS TO DO GUERRILLA THEATRE:
First off, research your topic inside out and from beginning to end:
Go to the internationally concerned and committed agencies like Indochina Peace Committee, Veterans Against The War, American Friends Service Committee, etc.
the card catalog of your nearest libraries
Stars and Stripes magazine (to get numbers of war dead)
newspapers from the right, middle, and left of the political spectrum
periodicals (like *Atlas* and *International Digest* which have articles from around the world)
After you have done your research and have compiled sufficient data
evaluate
compare
cross-compare all your material to insure its accuracy.

Now here are some scenarios in which you can
use your researched material to
guerrilla theatre effect.

(Remember they are offered not as the be-all and end-all of
guerrilla theatre but as possibilities to open up other
possibilities.)

PROTEST AGAINST NUCLEAR TESTING

Six people sing songs
     dance $\Big\}$ against war and for life.
     recite poems

Then with megaphones and in dry "objective" voices, the
actors recite data about Hiroshima and Nagasaki. They
describe what happened when the bomb hit and what has
happened biologically, neurologically, and psychologically to
the survivors.

In between each *substantiated* detail of the nuclear holocaust
an actor in a business suit says:
"Hello, General, this is General Motors (or Chase Manhattan
or AT&T or whatever multinational you choose). Our economy's in trouble. We need those problems solved in
Southeast Asia (or Guatemala, or Africa, or Detroit, or
whatever area is being sacked by the power elite)."

An actor in an army uniform responds:
"Wait till we get the go-ahead from Jimmy and Cyrus—we'll
solve those problems. We've got the final nuclear solution for
Southeast Asia or Detroit or Africa or wherever.")"

The piece ends with a stylized nuclear holocaust:
The sheets on which the opening poems and songs were
written are burned. In the rising flames there is a quick
piercing cry. Then silence. Over the devouring flames come
voices reciting the rise in gross national product during
wartime.

AT A CAMPUS DEMONSTRATION PROTESTING MILITARY RECRUITMENT AND/OR PENTAGON CONTRACTS

With the use of a bull-horn a mock interview is conducted with a larger-than-life academic:

INTERVIEWER: Tell me, professor, what do you think about this demonstration?

PROFESSOR: (With a condescending, studied smile) They're children. Still wet behind the ears. Immature. Give 'em a couple of years; they'll settle down, get a home and family. They'll forget trying to change the world once they're faced with real, down-to-earth problems.

INTERVIEWER: And the demonstration itself. What do you think about it?

PROFESSOR: The university is not the place for radicals. Calm inquiry, that's what we promote. I'm against all this violence.

INTERVIEWER: Do you call talking and standing and sign-carrying acts of violence?

PROFESSOR: I repeat. I'm against violence.

INTERVIEWER: What about the violence of unemployment, of starvation, of nuclear war?

PROFESSOR: Look, get off my back, I'm not a politician; I just teach. Let the government handle political issues.

INTERVIEWER: What do you teach?

PROFESSOR: Bio-chemistry.

INTERVIEWER: What about the Pentagon contracts given to universities for research in bio-chemical warfare?

PROFESSOR: I know nothing about that. I'm working on the sleeping habits of the queen bee. What are you talking about?

INTERVIEWER: I'm talking about bio-chemical warfare and the direct and indirect ways the government contracts universities to do research perfecting the uses of bio-chemical warfare.

PROFESSOR: Where's the proof of those assertions?

INTERVIEWER: Here are reports from the *New York Times* (data and page) *Newsweek* (data and page) and *Atlas*.

PROFESSOR: Well give them to me I would like to read them. But remember young wo/man there certainly have always been wars and there always will be wars. A study of history will show you that. It's terrible. I know. But that's the way things are and we've got to be prepared.

INTERVIEWER: And a study of the present will show you that a war now would destroy civilization. Today is unlike the past. Your old, easy to teach slogan "history repeats itself" won't work anymore. Get something new to teach. Try the realities of today's world for a change. Or don't you believe students should know anything about the relevant issues of the day?

PROFESSOR: Well, of course.

INTERVIEWER: Well, nuclear power is relevant.

PROFESSOR: But let those young people deal with nuclear war in a spirit of calm. Let them write letters to their congressman. Do it the American way.

INTERVIEWER: And suppose writing letters to congresspeople doesn't work, as it mostly doesn't?

PROFESSOR: Well, you can say you tried.

INTERVIEWER: How do you personally feel about nuclear testing?

PROFESSOR: Well, I try to keep an open, objective view on this and all issues. But, of course I don't believe in nuclear testing or nuclear warfare. Not for a moment. But I feel we must be prepared. We must arm ourselves to the teeth if we are going to preserve peace in the world.

The interview continues as singers start to sing softly "Which Side Are You On?"

PROTEST AGAINST CONTINUED U.S. SUP—
PORT OF JUNTA IN CHILE (OR WHEREVER)

8-feet-tall puppet people with the faces of leading figures in the military-industrial-government-establishment.

(Actors use their own legs and feet; the papier-mache' puppet figure extends from the actor's waist on up. Eyes and mouths will be cut in appropriate places and appropriately concealed.)

The puppet people will talk to themselves and also dart in and among the crowd, jawboning and shaking hands.

Here's a sample dialogue (the figures are whoever the current President and Secretary of State are. Obviously the figures can change and the dialogue with them.)

PRESIDENT: Well, Mr. Secretary, just remember what's good for ITT is good for the country. Now we've got half an hour before I'm due in Pennsacola for an off-the-cuff, non-campaigning speech before November's presidential election. Let's have a cup of coffee. Whoops! Sorry, I spilled that on your new suit. Hard to know these days which is more expensive to replace, the coffee or the suit.

SECRETARY: I'll bet on the coffee. (Ha, ha.) But give me some with some of that eight-dollar-a-gallon milk. It'll pick me up so I can use the half-hour to solve the problems between Israel and the Arabs.

PRESIDENT: Oh, are they having problems? What's up?

SECRETARY: Economy.

PRESIDENT: Oh, is the economy up? I thought it was down a little.

SECRETARY: What I meant, Resident, I mean President, is that we need a new war, but not for four or five months. So here's what I'll do. I'll sell Israel more nuclear missiles without launching pads. Then I'll sell the Arabs launching pads without the missiles. That way we'll maintain peace in the Middle East till the exact right moment we need a war.

PRESIDENT: Who do we want to win, Israel or the Arabs?

SECRETARY: The United States.

PRESIDENT: Sounds good, Secretary, sounds good. By the way, how are things in Chile?

SECRETARY: AT and T is back in the saddle. We've wiped up that messy little Marxist puddle.

PRESIDENT: You're a good man, Secretary. How do you know how to do so much?

SECRETARY: How? Well, it's mainly because I'm brilliant, but also I've had a little help along the way. My parents gave me my I.Q. and class superiority as a natural birthright. My schoolmates and teachers in private schools gave me the incentive to compete and win. Harvard gave me the know-how of imperialism, and (wife's name) does my shirts.

BOYCOTT AGAINST NON—UNION GRAPES BEING DUMPED ON MARKETS FOR QUICK, CHEAP SALE.

6-60 people with home made instruments
2 people with guitars
1 person with drums
Each person has a statement "for the revolution"
The statements may come from George Jackson
Malcom X
Chavez
Fanon
Appalachia
Native Americans
Prisoners
Children.

The statements can be song
>dance
>scenes
>quotations.

Each statement is introduced by a rhythmical musical phrase from the people's band.
During rhythmic interludes a person comes forward in a stylized gait.
When the person is "stage front" everyone shouts in unison:
"Statement for the Revolution!"
The person recites the source of her/his statement,
and presents the song
>quotation
>poem
>dance for the revolution.

At the end of the presentation another phrase of people's music is played and all the players shout "Viva la Revolution!"
This round continues until all statements have been made.

CRIME TRIALS

Bertrand Russell, Jean Paul Sartre, et al., conducted a trial examining and condemning the atrocities committed by the French against the Algerians. In the proceedings France was put on trial and all her actions against the Algerians were detailed
>examined
>analyzed.

Witnesses were called
>examined
>cross-examined.

Finally, sentence was leveled.
In the same way a mock trial can be conducted examining
U.S. treatment of Native Americans
>Chicanos
>Blacks
U.S. treatment of Latin America
U.S. treatment of South East Asia
U.S. treatment of New York City

Detroit
Boston
or whatever metropolitan area from which the
wealthy have fled, and the poor are left to pay the
taxes, and deal with declining services and rising
crime.
ITT can be put on trial: its support of Hitler in the
Second World War, and of fascist governments
today in Chile and elsewhere can be examined.
The schools of this country can be put on trial, their
"educational" policies analyzed.
Prison ⎫
Hospital ⎬ institutions can be put on trial
Mental ⎭

All that is necessary to conduct the trials against any force you feel to
be contra-human is detailed
                              factual
                                 precise knowledge of the subject.

The trial procedure is simple
                              stark
                                 to the point
and makes for effective guerrilla theatre.

PROTEST AGAINST IMPERIALISM

From books
        newspapers
        American Friends Service Committee
get names of people and numbers of people who have died fighting
for their national sovereignty
against imperialism.

Make death masks.
On the foreheads put the number of deaths that each mask represents.
Four people play drums and funeral chimes.
As the drums and chimes sound,
one by one each person in a death mask

calls out the atrocity
s/he endured.
e.g., "I am Lin Tau. I'm one of 37 people who died in Laos, January 4,
    1973 in a napalm attack on my village. I was sixteen years old at
    the time you killed me."
On and on into the night
the roll call continues
as drums and chimes underscore
the dirge of human slaughter.

You now have half a dozen guerrilla theatre pieces for your use. All of
them—like the other scenarios in this book—can be modified to meet
the immediate needs of your group.

Remember, these scenarios are but a few of
limitless possibilities for guerrilla theatre.
Your own passion and
the passion of your community
will tell you when
        how
        where
you may wish to make
outcries in the theatre
      against injustice in the world.

FOOTNOTES
1. Albert Camus, *The Rebel, Alfred A. Knopf, 1954, p.19.*

10
MAKING AN HONEST PERSON
OUT OF THEATRE

By acts of commission and omission our theatre has injured women, the long-living, Indians, Spanish-speaking, farmers, laborers, and Blacks. There are no scripted female or Black Hamlets; the long-living, if they appear in a play at all, are not usually wise but quaint—like an attic relic looked at once every 5 years or tossed out altogether; Puerto Ricans whose struggle for independence in their own country, as well as their struggle for survival in this one, constitutes an epic of heroic proportions are seen on our stage as grocery boys or explosively undulating singers. In the People's Republic of China, rather than fairy tales about princesses, the young see their own likeness in the theatre in stories about the daughters and sons of bakers and plumbers and farmers. The majority of young in our country, as well as the middle-aged and long-living, seldom see their own likeness. Instead, they are asked to measure themselves against the fakely witty, the beautiful, the powerful, the rulers, and heir apparents of our glitteringly acquisitive kingdom.

In sum, much of our Western theatre has been anti-human in its classism, sexism, racism, and ageism. There are exceptions, of course, but they don't spring readily to mind.

134

QUESTION: What to do, then, when your theatre wants to do a particular play and an analysis of it reveals that it is anti-human on one, maybe many, counts?

ANSWER: Make the play pro-human on all counts.

Before looking at ways to transform traditional theatre into a theatre that is for the people, a cautionary word is in order: begin this conversion process with a play whose basic philosophy

politics and

passion you respect.

Two wrongs don't make a right so never change any play wantonly or quixotically, never change for the sake of change. Change only for the sake of people and, even then, exercise great custodial care from the moment you start until you complete your humanizing work.

Significantly, when such respectful changes in the people's favor are made, the resulting production can remain faithful to the spirit—if not the exact letter—of the piece.

QUESTION: If one basically respects the play and is troubled only by occasional anti-humanisms in it, why bother to change it at all? Do the piece for what it is and let the chips fall where they may. After all, theatre's art and art doesn't really affect people's behavior, right?

ANSWER: Wrong. There is no such thing as neutral art. The American Indian movement said recently that the criminal treatment of Native Americans in this country is due not only to economic greed of the ruling class but to the way Indians are portrayed in movies, T.V., and the theatre. Blacks, Chicanos, women, and the aged have all leveled similar justifiable charges at the "entertainment" media. No. Letting the chips fall where they may has allowed too many to fall on the heads of the oppressed. It's high time we changed that. It's high time everyone in theatre—and out of it—take responsibility for creating a new situation, one which makes possible the pursuit of a fuller humanity for all people.

QUESTION: What to do about a play that has anti-humanisms in it but the author won't allow any changes to be made—or you feel that making the necessary changes will destroy the intention of the work?

ANSWER: Do another play.

This understood, let's get on to what we can do to change the all-too-prevalent situation of anti-humanism in the theatre. But before all purists seize this book and destroy it for its assertion that one dare tamper with the words of the play, rest assured that very few suggestions about to be made involve changing the script more than a few words—if there are any word changes at all. Moreover, let's face it, scarcely a production gets on the boards that doesn't involve a word change here and there, usually because such changes would benefit either the credibility or the theatricality of the piece. The humanity of the piece, I submit, is an equally important reason for change.

I will now cite specific insults to the people in traditional theatre and discuss ways these insults can be dealt with when directing traditional plays or when writing people's plays. The point is now for us all to learn from one another how to make the theatre a place where all people can see their full potential. For such opening up of the possibilities can be the quintessential joy of the theatre experience. It is an especially fruitful joy in that once people see their potential *in* the theatre, they stand a far greater chance of realizing it *out* of the theatre.

QUESTION: Why should theatre affect life off the stage? Isn't theatre, as Shakespeare said, "A mirror that reflects reality"?

ANSWER: (in two parts)

(1) To show the genuine life possibility of all people instead of only the kings, queens, and financially endowed heir apparents *is* to mirror reality rather than reflect an elitist, manipulative concept of it.

(2) Even more significantly, theatre can go beyond Shakespeare's concept. It can be, as Tolstoy said, not just a mirror that reflects "but a hammer that shapes reality."

Now to discuss specific insults of traditional theatre and their possible remedies in people's theatre.

INSULT TO THE PEOPLE: THE STAR AND INDIVIDUALISM

In so much Western theatre,
one person shines: the hero
                  the divinely
                       aesthetically or
                       financially   chosen one.

The rest, the supernumeraries, either get reflected light, or they are banished to that anonymous darkness which is the fate of the "rank and file" in non-people's theatre.

QUESTION: What to do to discourage this individualism which casts one person in the controlling, enviable limelight and pits the other "bit" players against each other (as if to practice for that same competitive round once the play is over and the other, real thing outside the theatre resumes)?

ANSWER: Nothing totally compensates for star theatre but the least we can do is divide the role of the hero so there are heroes.

For instance, the title role in Camus' *Caligula* can be divided. Due to the complexity of the man, the division easily offers itself:
a man (black) can play the central, public Caligula
a woman (white) can play his interior, private self
three people (two women and a man) can play mirrored aspects of this absurdly self-conscious ruler.

QUESTION: How can dividing the role of Caligula benefit people and the play?

ANSWER: The division makes protagonists out of one protagonist. Allows for the theatrical showing of more facets of this complex person.
Gives parts to five performers where normally one would have been cast.
Gives parts to four women where none would have been cast.

Caligula

Albert Camus

from *Tania* by Maxine Kle

Allows **Black** and white, men and women, to unite
together to play one person, showing thereby, that the
human similarities uniting us are greater than any class,
race, or sex differences that divide us.
**Opens up exciting new staging possibilities as five
people can be sculpted into one.**

In *Tania* (a play about the worker-woman, Tamara Bunke), the
title role was written in such a way that it could be played by two
women.

QUESTION: What did the two Tania's give the staged experience that
only one could not have?

ANSWER: It made **Tania's** acts less the result of one person's
courage and commitment and, more realistically, the
result of everyone's. Let me give an example of the
realism of this seemingly unrealistic device. At the end
of the play—as at the end of Tania's life—she fights as a
foot soldier in Che Guevara's last campaign in Bolivia,
and she is killed. On stage one Tania died, but the other
lived on to continue the struggle. In a very real sense,
this is what happened in real life. When Che and Tania
were killed, their comrade Inti and his comrades fought
on in the Bolivian jungles for another 7 years before
being caught and killed. And their struggle, in turn, was
continued by others. One person doesn't make or break
the movement (unlike John Wayne movies). There are
always others to take their place.

Another benefit—exclusively ethical—of dividing and
thus demystifying heroic roles should be noted. In the
theatre, as in life, when heroes are cut down to their
proper human size, the rest of the people become
stronger. They become stronger precisely because they
are not asked to look at the hero and exclaim "what an
extraordinary human being: I could never be like that!"
Instead, they are lead to say "this is a great person. But
s/he is a person after all, not a demi-god. I could be like
that if I tried."

from *Approaching Simone* by Megan Te...

This concept of dividing the central character is not new. Paul Baker used three Hamlets; the Firehouse Theatre in Minneapolis staged *Peer Gynt* with a number of Peers. Megan Terry's *Approaching Simone* was performed with two Simones and can use over thirty people to play her emotional moods and philosophic ideas. And, lest it be misunderstood, all these productions kept their comprehensibility, interest, and theatricality even though they divided the central character. To the same extent that they offered more roles to actors and demystified heroes, the productions became more human, more interesting, and more theatrical.

INSULT TO THE PEOPLE: SMALL CASTS

Too many plays call for small casts, some as small as 2 to 4 people.

QUESTION: What to do for all the actors who have to sit on the sidelines watching the chosen few do their work?
ANSWER: Either divide the roles that do exist among more people; double the cast; or do a different play—one that uses the talent, imagination and energy of more people.

INSULT TO THE PEOPLE: RACISM

Except in plays written by members of minorities, themselves, most Western plays picture minorities as stereotypical objects of the ruling class—if, indeed, minorities are pictured at all.

QUESTION: What to do when no minorities are called for in a play or when the minority roles are written as stereotypes?
ANSWER: Cast against color and against stereotype.

In Camus' *Caligula*, the intellectual ruler can be cast as a black man precisely because blacks are too infrequently cast as intellectual giants. The congress and military, however, can be cast in such a way that neither color nor sex are issues. Black, white, and chicano men and women can play actions not prejudices.
In *Fanshen*, a play about the revolution in China, Blacks, whites, and Chinese can be cast as the villagers of Long Bow, China. Nothing should be made of their race; it is their class struggle that is the issue.
In *Tania*, a Black and white woman together can play the central

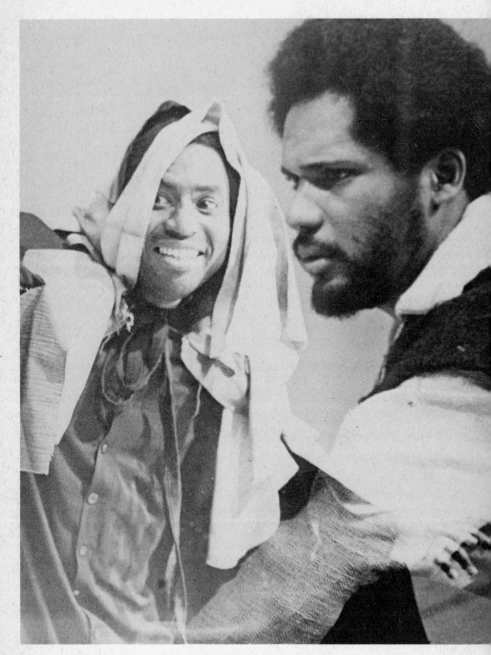

from *Blood Wedding* by Garcia Lorc

character, Tania; a Black man can play Fidel; a Black and white man can share the part of Che; and a Black and white woman can share the role of Tania's mother.

Another possibilty of confronting racism in the theatre is to cast in such a way that the tragedy of racism is central to the play's action. In Garcia Lorca's *Blood Wedding*, the family conflict at the center of the play can be a racial conflict, one family can be Black, one white. The ultimate tragedy that evolves, therefore, is one in which racism plays its deadly role.

INSULT TO THE PEOPLE: SEXIST, RACIST, ANTI-HUMAN LANGUAGE

QUESTION: What to do when a play's language insults minorities either for the sake of diversion or "unconsciously" (not for the sake of illuminating the viciousness of such lauguage)?

ANSWER: Get rid of such language. The plays will not suffer the loss of a word or two. Neither, as a result of those words, will women, Blacks, the long-living, and other human beings in the cast and audience increase their suffering.

INSULT TO THE PEOPLE: AGEISM

As valuable as it is to cast Blacks, Native Americans and other minorities, it is also equally valuable to cast the long-living—one of the most oppressed of all minorities in this country. But when you cast the long-living, don't cast them in roles that ridicule age. Quite the reverse: cast them in roles that require wisdom, a sense of humor, and life and spirit. In other words, cast them as they are, not as the cruel media has depicted them.

If it takes a while to find long-living people to be in your theatre, it's worth the effort. And this, not only for the audience, many of whom will be long-living and need to see their genuine likeness on stage, but also for the cast. There is so much to be learned from our brothers and sisters who have lived long lives. So much. And this age-race-sex segregated society too often prevents that necessary education.

from *Fanshen* by David Hare

from *Approaching Simone* by Megan Te

It would, incidently, be interesting to see what would happen to the quality of life of the aged in this country if the media started treating them as human beings rather than castaways. We have all seen and read enough to know in what hovels we force the majority of the long-living to end their days. I submit that every time we ignore and treat the aged viciously on stage, we contribute to that inhuman sensibility which condones this national disgrace. Ironically, in so doing, we mock our own possibilities, our own destiny.

Another aspect of ageism in the theatre is one that is suffered by the young as well as the old. It derives from the fact that the overwhelming majority of theatres in this country age-segregate their audience: children go to one show

> young adults to another
> the old folks stay home or in institutions.

A joyous rule of people's theatre is: let us do plays that young people, people of 98, and all in between can enjoy without boredom or embarrassment. Let our theatre be a place where families can come together to recognize and affirm the larger, human family.

(I have never done plays in which there were not young, middle-aged, and long-living who attended. Nor has this meant that I do simple-minded fairy tales. Quite the reverse. Almost all my plays have been ideological and to understand their ideology takes thought. To make these thought-provoking plays suitable and appealing for all ages, I avoid lurid sexuality and mindless violence, and I keep the plays as active, as spectacle and music-filled as possible.)

Now, to be sure, a young audience member's grasp of the play will probably be different from an older person's (not greater or lesser, just different). The point is to make sure there is something for all ages to grasp. SO OUR THEATRE can be an experience by families of people for families of people.

INSULT TO THE PEOPLE: SEXISM

If women were in real life what they are represented to be on most stages, T.V. shows, and in most movies in this country, they would be looked after in the day and penned up at night. From *Gentlemen Prefer Blondes* to *Gingerbread Lady* to "I'm Just a Girl Who Can't Say

No," theatre has created a mutant, put a skirt on it, and called it woman.

QUESTION: What to do when plays treat women as mindless bodies or neurotic-without-men careerists or biological sub-species?

ANSWER:　As with the long-living and workers and people of color either find plays that portray women as people, or don't do the plays, or adapt them.

INSULT TO THE PEOPLE: INTIMIDATING DISPLAYS OF WEALTH

By necessity, but also by choice, the theatre that most of us in the people's movement end up doing is poor theatre. Poor theatre asks that the audience imagine, fill in what the theatre experience evokes rather than spell it out with elaborate sets, costumes, and properties.

Tania had one property: dowels (at the cost of 75¢ each). The dowels became trains, guns, trees, houses, surreal webs, ballet bars—whatever was called for.

Tania's stage setting was one platform.

Fanshen had one property: a kettle (a found object; hence no cost). The kettle became the fire, a baby basket, a pot of food— whatever was needed at the moment.

Fanshen's stage setting consisted of 6 platforms.

Touch Kiss had no properties, no stage setting. Everything was mimed.

Blood Wedding had no properties. A simple practical background piece was used for the set.

All these plays were directed so that they could be performed in all kinds of rooms including, but not limited by, a formal theatre.

One soon discovers that audiences don't need—or even want—to be shown everything. One soon discovers that audiences don't need— or even want—a theatre whose plush seats and imposing stage intimidates them.

What audiences need to see is their own lives

passion

> destiny
> struggles
> possibilities staged in an
> exciting way

Give them this and they will gratefully, willingly create whatever you don't have the time

> money or
> inclination to create.

And, more significantly, not only will audiences create what you ask of them but, nine times out of ten, they'll do you one better.

QUESTION: Is it really the task of the theatre to make itself accessible to audiences? Is not our task to do art? If so, let's bring the audience up to our level: let's not lower ourselves to theirs.

ANSWER: I'll let Leo Tolstoy answer that oft-heard rhetorical question designed to justify elitist theatre. He said:

"For the great majority of working people, our art, besides being inaccessible on account of its costliness, is strange in its very nature, tansmitting as it does the feelings of people far removed from those conditions of laborious life which are natural to the great body of humanity. That which is enjoyment to a person of the rich classes is incomprehensible as a pleasure to a working person, and evokes in her/him either no feelings at all or only a feeling contrary to that which it evokes in an idle and satiated person...But if art is an important matter, a spiritual blessing, essential for all people...then it should be accessible to everyone. And if, as in our day, it is not accessible to all people, then one of two things: either art is not the vital matter it is represented to be or that art which we call art is not the real thing."[1]

I rest my case.

Let's do the "real thing."
Let's do theatre for the people.

FOOTNOTES

1. Leo Tolstoy, *What is Art?*, Bobbs and Merrill Co., 1960, p.70.

11
A PEOPLE'S THEATRE
CONTRACT

We theatre people live in the same society as everyone else. We are subject to all of its oppressions, to all of its molding and cajoling like everyone else. We are not perfect people. We are, because of our conditioning, sometimes egotistical and competitive, sometimes thoughtless, sometimes racist, sexist, or classist. We can be irresponsible, elitist, or overbearing. This means that when we work together things can become very complicated. There can be misunderstandings and pain. To work well together for long periods, to develop on-going people's theatre in a society that pushes us almost always toward bitter individualism is a struggle. We do not always, every minute, agree on the methods of that struggle, and we do not always succeed.

Recognizing our own fallibility and the pressures that will constantly be brought to bear upon us from without and within, and recognizing particularly the harm that can be done by misunderstandings, confused expectations, and selfish, or otherwise less than people's behavior, we call for a contract to help us through tougher times. Moreover, we call for a written contract, all the while recognizing that words on paper, no matter how well-thought-out and carefully articulated are but half measures. They can never substitute for ideological commitment manifesting itself in good, hard work towards valid theatre.

Granted if the theatre group is to be shortlived, if it arises to meet one particular production and then disbands, the full contract may not be so essential: the fervor of the group may be bond enough to maintain a single event. But longer term theatre groups need long term contracts. Reality has proven that no matter how in tune with one another people may appear at the start of a venture, as time, poverty, and hard work take their toll, problems can and often do arise. And these problems have TNT potential. They can shatter the solidest of groups into tiny fragments. So it is best to be forearmed with a contract agreed to in the calm of careful collective deliberation, the aim of which must be to protect both the individual members of the theatre and the theatre itself. And it is most important to note from the outset that those two sets of needs, though ultimately complimentary, do not always seem one and the same, especially in moments of conflict and particularly because of pressures from the society around us.

Following is a sample contract. It is presented as a guide emerging from a particular complex of experiences and of course you should modify it to fit your own situation. But reaching some shared understanding of guiding principles, of expectations, of plans, and of how the group will work together to overcome its own failings and external problems is crucial. Real hard experience will, of course, continually modify the group's understandings and the written contract which concretely expresses those understandings, but at all times such understanding and contract, however flexible, must be explicit.

Leadership Guidelines

Sometimes a division of labor makes good sense. In a factory where the division of labor is aimed to reduce the individual's integrity to the barest minimum, it is always fragmenting. But in a people's organization this need not be so.

In a theatre group not everyone can always be doing everything. There has to be some division of tasks and responsibilities. At any moment, some person or persons must have coordinating responsibility for seeing to it that the aims of the group are effectively accomplished and that the needs of the group are met in as unified and mutually beneficial a way as possible. Theatre is by its very nature a collection of art and artisan forms. If all these elements are to be fused into one meaningful whole, some coordinator's vision is needed—typically that of the artistic director (or directors, if there are more than one).

The directorship must be able to excite, to use, to feed into and off of the suggestions and contributions of others. But, to repeat, unless that directorship fuses all the contributions into one artistic and ideological pattern, chaos results. And chaos can be at least as confusing, regressive, and selfishly individualist in theatre as in politics.

Now there is a difference between responsible leadership which coordinates many diverse elements into a whole and hierarchical usurpation. Leadership must mean responsibility not privilege. But to protect against leadership becoming privilege and hierarchy, and to protect against the theatre members being badly directed in their artistry and/or ideology, it must be understood that the directorship can be dismissed if it/they cease to serve the genuine, stated interests of the group, and that the directorship should be intelligently rotated with new people carefully learning the involved skills from those who already have more experience. Only with such a recall system and patient spreading of skills can the groups be safeguarded from hierarchical usurpation—which even the best intentioned leadership can fall sway to.

Rotation of Directorship and Other Tasks

In our society work is debilitating for many reasons. People's efforts are exploited with the profits going to the owners aimply because they own. But this is not the whole of the problem. Work in our society is also "alienated." We who do the work do not control it. Its product, process, and pace are determined by others. Our work stands against us, as an obstacle to get by, rather than as an end to be enjoyed for its own worth.

In people's theatre both for our own development *and as a model of people's possibilities,* we should try to make our work as human as possible.

We accomplish this partial'y by having responsive, recallable leadership, wages according to effort and need, and mutually decided and agreed upon purposes and policies.

But there is another difficult practice which can greatly aid the people's theatre's struggle toward human work. For part of the problem with work as we usually know it, is that it is static and boring. We do the same (usually minutely parcelled) things over and over. We are thus divided one from each other, and each from the whole project. No one, except perhaps the "boss," is aware of the whole process, and the boss's awareness is only intellectual, that of the overseer, not that of the participant. Each worker has knowledge of only one task and thus no real sensitivity to the efforts of her/his fellow workers. Each worker has tasks and responsibilities of only one kind, which develop only one set of skills, enrich only one side of life.

This permanent fragmentation and narrowing of human activity serves a purpose in the society around us. It keeps workers separated and thus weak. It denies them knowledge of the whole project and thus of the fact that they could do without the owner and boss. But this is a negative purpose which we needn't and shouldn't mimic in our people's theatre (nor in any of the people's institutions we will one day establish throughout our society).

As workers we want to have the greatest knowledge of each other's actions, to always take informed initiatives, to develop all-sidedly—we can't have everyone doing everything all the time but we can have a regular, well-planned, careful rotation. We can work to have people teach each other skills, share experiences, and carefully rotate tasks.

Just as no one person should always play the lead, and no one person always be the comic; also no one person should always direct, and no one person always handle publicity or finances. A job repeated ad-infinitum, even to a good mutually agreed upon end, eventually loses its interest and especially its worth as a vehicle of self-development. The old phrase that "variety is the spice of life," properly understood, has a profound truth about it. Tasks and responsibilities should be rotated.

But this doesn't mean that someone who has never directed should all too suddenly be called upon to single-handedly direct a play, nor that someone who has never done bills is suddenly handed the finance books, nor that an actor is asked to do comedy when she or he is simply not yet ready to. Rotation is aimed to develop skills, variety, collectivity, and understanding, not to destroy them. People must be prepared for their tasks. They should work and learn from those who know, becoming confident before adopting full responsibility for something new. This takes much time and effort but it is far from inefficient. It leads to more people contributing more originality to the whole theatre. The vitality of everyone's efforts is enhanced. Rotation promotes variety, mutual understanding and respect, initiative, more kinds of creativity, and an on-going living excitement due to people constantly learning and developing themselves and one another.

But like most other "people's policies" rotating tasks and responsibilities is initially quite difficult. It goes against many ingrained habits and can even be a little threatening to people's sense of where they fit and of their previously "permanent role." It can be carried to ridiculous self-defeating extremes. It must be practiced patiently, with great care and a sensitivity to pitfalls. But with practice, in time rotation, like sharing, becomes much more natural—for indeed it does correspond to the many sidedness and sociability we all have in common—and its human rewards can be undeniably immense, both for the theatre's actors and its audience.

Manifesto Guidelines

As important as good leadership and careful rotation are to people's theatre, so is a clearly stated manifesto. It is imperative that the group agree to and then state its ideological and artistic principles up front. Then, if for any reason the directorship or membership fails to agree with and/or carry out this manifesto, appropriate recall steps can be taken. But without a clearly stated manifesto all attempts to improve will be confused and invariably marked by severe misunderstandings.

Little Flags, for example, dedicates itself to a society free from oppression by race, by sex, by sexual preference, and by class. This manifesto makes the group openly political and asks that its members and directorship and their artistic product serve these political ends.

Little Flags also asserts that it's impossible to turn people on to ideas of social justice with dull stage work. So it demands high artistic quality in all its productions. This means Little Flags must have membership and directorship whose political commitment is equalled by and informed with artistic expertise.

Other groups may dedicate themselves to local folklore, community celebration, story-telling for and by the long-living. Some theatres may be more concerned about enriching the lives of their membership (theatre in unions, factories, prisons) than with artistic quality. *All such purposes are equally worthy.* The important thing is that the purpose be mutually defined and agreed to by all members and then clearly stated up front. Then everything possible must be done by the group to realize their stated goals.

Economic Guidelines

The economics of a people's theatre should be equal pay for equal work or payment according to greatest need of the worker. While the egalitarian ideal is difficult to attain, it should none-the-less be the goal. It is a safe and sure blow to the old hierarchical economic order which has dominated Western theatre for centuries. In that elitist-serving hierarchy, it is not quantity of labor or need of the laborer, but the character of labor that determines value. Thus it is assumed that the king-playwright gets the lion's share of the proceeds followed, but not too closely by the composer, the director, actors, designers—then come the technicians and last of all "unskilled labor." (Unless a "star" is involved in any of the categories; then it is fruit basket upset with the star ending up on top of the heap and others placed in their appropriate stellar-supportive positions.) Now to the notion that the playwright or director or star is the only "quality" person on whose contribution the success of the effort depends, and that everyone else deserves less because their contribution is not essential, we say, take the idea to its extreme limit and live with it. We say dismiss the "inessential" people and let the "quality" personnel go it alone. But if— after an hour or two of this—it is decided that the king and star cannot do all the theatre work alone, and that other people accordingly must be hired, then these people must be paid for their time. And their time is no more, no less important than anyone else's.

To the end of equal pay for equal work, we say that whenever possible, all the personnel should be paid equally. But, as happens from time to time, when added responsibility falls on certain people, those people must be compensated. For example, it is altogether possible, when theatre funds are low, that some members of the group can get jobs in the mornings and/or afternoons to supplement their theatre earnings. Other theatre members, however, might have to be on the job all the time, i.e. group sales and tour directors. If their being at the job prohibits their getting other work, then these people must be paid for the added burden they are assuming for the theatre's success.

Finances And The Treasurer

The person in charge of the finances, the treasurer, must be listened to; his/her regulations must be strictly followed. A poor theatre can nickel and dime itself to death in short order unless stringent financial guidelines are followed. To this end: .

a voucher system can be devised for all financial transactions.
a budget must be drawn up for each area of the theatre.
financial records must be kept of every financial transaction.
dates will be determined for the payment of wages, bills, etc.
checks must be ready on the agreed upon date.
everyone should scout around for free props, costumes, and set pieces.
all necessary purchases should be made with the approval of the production coordinator.

Other Employment:

We have to talk about paying jobs. Most people's theatres are composed of working people who don't live off the sweat of others but who must make their own way. It is hoped that when paying jobs are offered to any member, that member will do everything in his/her power to schedule it at a time that doesn't conflict with rehearsals. However, if it becomes a question of not getting the needed job or going to rehearsal, it is expected that the theatre will do everything in its power to make the necessary adjustments so that the member can take the job. Of course, if the success of the theatre becomes jeopardized by people taking outside work—granted not because of selfishness but human need—a meeting will have to be held and the situation discussed, and appropriate actions taken.

The Publicist And Publicity Guidelines

That person who has charge of publicity both in town and on the road holds one of the most important positions in people's theatre. Only if the word gets out to the people, will they come to the event. But it is important that the word get out in a way that conforms to the artistic and ideological view of the show. This is to say that we never want publicity for the sake of or justified by the view of commerce. It must be publicity for people's theatre's sake. It must spread the word that a show of, for, and about the people exists. And the work should be said in such a way that all the people who hear it will want to come to *their* show.

While certain people will be centrally responsible for publicity, everyone must be available to help. This means everyone will:

advertise the show to friends, acquaintances, and any and all potential audience members.

be available for interviews.

put up posters, and when they are torn down, put them up again.

seek out groups (high schools, factories) which have audiences who might like the show, and discuss the show with them.

be available to advertise the show on special occasions (i.e., singing the songs from the show and handing out posters and literature in public places).

be available for group mailings, phone calls, and whatever publicity tasks may arise.

Practical and Aesthetic Guidelines

1. Stay healthy and keep your body and vocal equipment in good shape.

2. Have spirit and attention for the work to be done. Creativity doesn't happen automatically; it must be fed and nurtured like any living, growing thing. If one member treats rehearsal and/or group meetings as something to be endured, his/her negativity infects the entire group. Creativity falters, bickering begins; theatre ends.

3. Join in the continuing process of developing constructive, non-threatening dialogue. The assumption of a people's theatre is that an idea which evolves from or is modified by many is sounder, richer than any one person's idea. To this end, in our aesthetic and organizational development, we must feed off one another's contribution. One method is to remain flexible about one's own ideas and to avoid a flat out "No" to someone else's. With such cooperative tools we pave the way for a productive dialectic. So:

> Carefully think through and advance your ideas (remember, being a member of a people's theatre does not give you the freedom not to think).
>
> Let your ideas be modified by other's advice.
>
> The group work that evolves will, hopefully, contain the best of everyone's offering.

We must be advised, however, that in this group process, personal expertise is to be respected and safeguarded, but not deferred to. And it should also be shared wherever possible. Thus, a people's theatre calls for a delicate balance between personal expertise and group modification. If we are genuinely committed to excellent theatre, that balance can evolve organically.

4. Don't resist change. The people's theatre dialectic suggests, is founded on change. Theatre rehearsal is a time of evolution. Theatre's most carefully laid out plans are advanced, modified, and if necessary, modified again and again until the best theatre that we are capable of is achieved.

5. No one member of the people's theatre is a servant to anyone else. The people's theatre is founded in direct opposition to hierarchy. All members and all tasks are no more or no less important than any other. All members should take it as their task to understand, value, and assist the others in their area of expertise. In this way, each person and part of our theatre can be actualized as fully as our time, money, energy, and production aesthetic will allow.

6. Do your private work. Each of us—the playwright, publicist, actor, technicians, etc. has extensive private work to do outside the rehearsal. Rehearsal is the time to bring together everyone's private work so it can be modified and grow and find its full life in the complex and interactive production pattern. But remember, nothing can grow unless there is seedling and spade work.

Procedural Guidelines

It is important that your contract include procedures for the specific running of rehearsals, performances, auditions, meetings, etc. In each case the previous criteria of rotation and skill-sharing should be kept in mind.

For instance:

Running the show: each person in the collective will take a task. One or two people should be responsible for the following areas:

    vocal warm-ups
    physical warm-ups
    song warm-ups
    setting and striking props and costumes
    setting up the front of the house
    cleaning the stage and house before and after the show
    talking to interested people and groups after the show.

Your theatre will, of course, evolve its own guidelines for working and developing collectively. But if you want your theatre to survive, grow, and flourish

DRAW UP A CONTRACT FOR YOUR GROUP

12
A PEOPLE'S
THEATRE NETWORK

QUESTION: There are very few jobs in theatre
for very many people.
How do I find work?
ANSWER: Start a theatre and hire yourself.
QUESTION: Who will pay me?
ANSWER: 1. If you start a theatre which puts on stage
the genuine concerns of the people in this country
and if you do that theatre excitingly
people will come to see you.
What's more,
they will pay a reasonable admission price.
(Better said, those who can pay will pay; for those who
can't, the theatre must lower its prices.)
Subtract the theatre costs from the admission monies
and, hopefully, you will have something left over
to profit-share.

2. While the aim of a people's theatre should be full economic support for all its members, initially, theatre can operate in such a way that it is possible for at least some, and maybe all, of its members to maintain other jobs. Operating this way will not place the too-heavy burden of supporting a full group of actors and technicians on a still fledgling theatre. What is important, however, is that the people's theatre always works toward the goal of full economic support for all its members.

(Look at it this way: a plumber should not support his/her work in plumbing by being forced to take outside employment, say as a restaurant worker or a taxi driver. Neither should an actor have to support his/her work in theatre by taking outside jobs. A cultural worker's labor is no less and no more important and time consuming than any other worker's labor; consequently the cultural worker deserves no less and no more economic compensation for labor expended than any other laborer on any other job.)

3. Another way for people's theatre members to support themselves is to share all the money each member makes—not only *inside* but *outside* the theatre. Thus, whenever one actor makes money teaching, driving a taxi, waiting on tables, cleaning house, etc. s/he puts that money in a common fund from which all members are paid at the end of every week. In this way, if the theatre cannot pay a living wage from its box office alone, and if someone is temporarily without an outside job, s/he can be assured of support until a job comes along. Also, if the theatre demands that some of its members devote full time to the theatre while others supplement their income with an outside job, those members working full time at the theatre are assured of a maintenance salary.

(The Next Move Theatre in Boston has been

operating in this manner for four years. And it has
served this theatre well—not without an occasional hitch, but so well that they plan to continue this
way indefinitely.)

4.   A fourth avenue of support for your theatre is
benefit performances. When a political/educational
group has a pressing financial need, and when that
group's passion and ideology are complimentary with a
people's cultural group, the two organizations can
combine their efforts and give a benefit performance:

> Both groups dramatize their concerns.
> Both groups reach a wider audience than they
> would have otherwise.
> Both groups gain from profit-sharing one
> another's ideas as well as from the proceeds of the
> benefit performance.

5.   A fifth and most effective collective avenue of
support for your theatre is to form alliances with other
members of the people's movement so that you can
mutually benefit each other.

> Boston's Living Newspaper operates out of the
> Red Book Store. Both people's organizations serve
> and are served by the other's presence, ideology,
> and economics.
> Boston's Newbury Street Theatre operates oc-
> casionally out of The Community Church of
> Boston. Each contributes to the other's welfare
> and enlarges the audience of the other. And one of
> the Newbury Street Theatre's productions was
> given space by the Harvard School of Public
> Health because the play was about an occupation-
> al health issue: the dangers of poly vinyl chloride.
> Boston's Littie Flags is sharing space with the
> People's Theatre.

(The list of such alliances in the people's movement around the country could go on and on. But however many alliances there are in however many cities, all of us in the people's movement still have a long way to go before we learn how to support each other. In a society that has taught us individualism and competition from birth to casket-choosing, it is not easy suddenly to think collectively; it's harder yet to trust that thinking once it starts; and it's hardest of all to act on that thinking.)

QUESTION: If our group follows all the above guidelines, can we be assured of our theatre's providing us a living wage?

ANSWER: No.

QUESTION: If our group follows the above guidelines, can we be assured of substantial economic support?

ANSWER: A conditional, "yes." That condition being that the people's cultural group must not only do work that is responsive to the needs of the people of this country; it must do it well: people culture must not be less but more exciting than establishment culture. And why not? After all, our subject matter, passion, reason for being and our audience are more exciting than the establishment's. Why shouldn't our culture be also?

QUESTION: For both ideological and economic reasons, people's cultural groups want to reach the widest possible audience. When the group doesn't have a lot of time to spend on advertising, how does it get the word out? How, in effect, does it let people know that it exists and has something to offer?

ANSWER: 1. Send newsletters to people's organizations advertising your existence and your dates, times, and place of performance.

2. Stand in the busiest sidewalks on their busiest days with placards advertising your event.

3. Attend meetings of organizations which you think might be interested in your group's productions, and either ask to address them, or, at least, leave printed

information explaining your group and its offerings.
4. Develop group sales mailing lists. One such campaign designed by Jayne Chamberlin is described in a letter she wrote to her people's organization. This letter should provide the most useful information about how to develop from scratch a group sales list.

Little Flags Mailing List Procedure

First of all, think of your work on this as a kind of sleuthing project. A correct mailing list for our theatre does not exist—we must develop it ourselves. This does not mean that you cannot use other lists already developed and work from them. But they are only a starting point and must be made particular for us.

Now, this is the sleuthing part: we want to find the groups of individuals in this city who belong to organizations, schools, church groups, etc., who would be interested on us, who need us as much as we need them. We are relevant to people who are into:

> Political theatre
> Experimental theatre
> Latin America
> China
> Appalachia
> Feminism
> American underground politics
> Other: you will find other handles of interest; when you
> do, write them down to share with the rest of us.

These are, hopefully, groups of people who will come en masse to our theatre, therefore, get a special discount rate. There are several different ways they can use the theatre event:
> 1. The group or college can simply use it to offer a discount to their group members and provide a group event.
> 2. The group can also use it as a fund raising event for themselves (i.e., we give them a discount, perhaps even sell out the house to them; they charge whatever they want for the tickets and keep the excess funds).

3. The theatre can meet with their group after the show for a discussion, etc., to make it more of an educaional or social event for them.

Later, we will determine how much discount for what size groups, etc. Now, our purpose is to get those names, addresses, phone numbers, groups, on a mailing list.

Here's how to do it:

Take an area and pursue it, probably sharing it with another person. You will want to make sure that efforts and calls do not overlap. When you call, try to talk with the person who could most effectively implement the two group's getting together. It is very important that you establish specific contact with at least one such person. That way, when you send information in your continuing negotiations, you can always address the same person. (Otherwise, with each call, you run the risk of having to re-explain what you have already explained in the past.)

Of course, it may not be you who will be doing future negotiations. So it is critically important that you get all the correct information on a card, including the contact person's name, correct address, all phone numbers at which s/he can be reached.

WHEN YOU CALL A GROUP:

1. Tell them who you are, tell them what your theatre is, tell them about your shows (their theatricality, politics, and passion).

2. Tell them you want to let them know about it in case their organization would like to come and get a discount, etc. They may not immediately give you the information you want, i.e., they may say they are interested but to not do things as groups. It is still worth it if they will put a notice on the bulletin board, mention the theatre at a meeting, publicize it in their newsletter. JUST MAKE SURE THAT YOU NOTE ON THE BACK OF THEIR CARD WHETHER THEY DO OR DO NOT ATTEND THINGS AS GROUPS. Then you will know to send them different information.

3. Find out if they have a newsletter. If yes, you will fill out another card about that.

4. VERY IMPORTANT: at the end of the conversation, ask if they know other people or groups that would be interested in what you are doing. Engage them in helping you. Get names and numbers from them.

5. You must be very organized and thorough in your information-gathering. If at all possible, type the information on cards. If you can't type, make sure your writing is legible.

This work is time consuming. It is also VITAL for the theatre!

QUESTION: If our group desires, how do we get the word out to national people's networks that we exist? This is particularly important, of course, if we want to perform our pieces throughout the nation.

ANSWER: Bill Castellino, an actor/choreographer/dancer/writer political activist, got the word out and subsequently designed a national tour. Because his entire plan worked so well, I will summarize it for you.

1. Collect the names of people's organizations, colleges, universities, and civic organizations sympathetic to people's culture from around the country.

This process involves more than leafing through the People's Yellow Pages—though it involves that, too. It involves making direct personal contact with people's organizations, particularly with those who would seem to be most responsive to your piece.

2. After you have assembled names and addresses, send a letter to each announcing that you exist and what you are about.

3. After a couple of weeks, send a brochure to those same people and organizations. In the brochure, describe your play's ideology and its theatricality.

4. Again, after two weeks, send another brochure, this one having a tear off sheet which anyone interested in your offering can send for additional information.

5. ONCE YOU RECEIVE THE TEAR OFF sheets, the real negotiations begin. Both you and your potential host will have agree on cost, dates, publicity etc.

All these negotiations take time, patience, compromise, mutual respect, and courtesy—and precision, precision, precision. But the end result is worth whatever time is expended.

6. After both you and the host organization have agreed on specifics, you must send a contract covering all the issues agreed upon and designed to protect both the performers and the host organization. The more specific the contract, the better. Remember, you could find yourselves miles from nowhere in the middle of a desert, little money in hand, and discover that the host organization had decided to cancel your performance. A well-written courteous and respectful contract protects you against such dire emergencies.

7. Once the contract is signed and returned, the tour approaches its final stage of readiness. That approach includes mutually agreed upon guidelines for day-to-day as well as performance procedures.

QUESTION: Isn't there a way to cut down on the work that is necessary to get the word out about your group, both locally and nationally?

ANSWER: Yes. A decided, yes!

An organized people's network is called for.

All its parts would know that each other part exists
where each other part exists
how to contact each other
part for information and/or
service.

All this so that all parts of the people's network can best serve and be served by all its other parts.

For the fact is that the need, one for the other, is as pressing as it is immediate and total.

The day must come in the not-too-distant future when we in the people's movement can get our
educational—medical—legal—spiritual—cultural
needs serviced by one another.

Then we can truly, totally boycott the cartel killers.
Until then, we're just whistlin' Dixie.
So what we need is a people's hotline, a vast filing service
fully staffed and financed by all the participants of the people's
movement.
This people's computer should be ready to give name

service
need
location

of all people's groups around the nation
to all people's groups around the nation.
We must not rest until this is done.

QUESTION: What kind of people are needed for doing people's
                theatre?
ANSWER:

They should be people who have expertise in their area (acting,
dancing, singing) but who are also willing and able to do the
million and one other things that their theatre asks of them—
from sweeping floors to organizing tours.

They should be people who are well-organized, because a people's
theatre is dependent on its organization, from rehearsals to
bookings to assembling lists of people's organizations. The
establishment theatres hire people for this work. People's
theatre does it themselves and takes pride in the fact that they
are their own laborers.

They should be people who are ideologically committed to doing
theatre about and with those people who are not normally the
subject of theatre in this country: the workers, Blacks, Spanish-
speaking, politicos, long-living, strong women, Native Americans.

They should be people committed to overcoming, on and offstage, the
competitive, self-oriented way of thinking and behaving that
characterizes performers in this country. In a profession which
has been geared to promoting the individual, "the star," such
thinking is not easy.

They should be people who are not harsh and judgemental with one
another but capable of struggling with one another's weaknesses
and rejoicing in one another's strengths.

They should be people who study and prepare outside the theatre so
that they understand thoroughly the content and implications
and responsibility of the dramas they are doing.

QUESTION: Isn't all this asking a lot of the people who choose to do
people's theatre?

ANSWER: Yes.

QUESTION: Is it worth it?

ANSWER: Yes.

Let Victor Jare, the Chilean folksinger, executed by
the military Junta in September, 1973, answer whether
or not a dedication to the people is worth extreme
sacrifice.

I am a person happy to exist
at this moment
Happy because
when one puts one's
heart, reason, and will
to work at the
service of the
people
one feels the happiness
of that which begins to
be reborn.[1]

FOOTNOTES

1. Victor Jare, from a pamphlet put out by San Francisco Non-Intervention in Chile,
    P.O. Box 6669, San Francisco, CA 94101.

South End Press is a collective of six activists committed to furthering a socialist movement in the United States. A part of this process is publishing books which can aid people's day-to-day struggles to control their lives. We seek to understand how the oppressions of race, sex, and class in the United States are perpetuated through the economic and political systems and in our culture, ideology, and consciousness.

We are striving for a world in which all people are directly and collectively in control of their lives. Because our publishing is aimed at developing widespread political awareness, our books are written, designed, and priced for accessibility. Our distribution will reach people's associations as well as traditional retail channels. To further the political use of our books, we will promote study groups, speaking engagements by authors, and cultural events.

We want to demystify the actual process of writing and publishing books. To overcome the traditional hierarchy and alienation, we involve authors as much as possible in the decisions and procedures concerning their books, and we solicit work from many people who would not ordinarily have access to a press.

By the kinds of books we publish and the methods we use, we hope to contribute to the improvement of the quality of daily life in the United States.

For more information about the press and its membership plan, please contact us at:

SOUTH END PRESS
Box 68, Astor Station
Boston, MA. 02123
tel. (617) 266-0629

MORE TITLES FROM SOUTH END PRESS

Ba Ye Zwa *by Judy Seidman.* Prints and sketches portraying the Black struggle against apartheid in South Africa. Commentary on the cold realities of day to day life, the culture, history and resistance.
Available: Dec. 1, 1977 $4.50—178 pp.

Conversations In Maine *by Grace Lee Boggs, James Boggs, Freddy Paine, and Lyman Paine.* A five year dialogue by four longtime social activists seeking to understand personal transformation and the roles of community and culture within a revolutionary process.
Available: Feb. 1, 1978 $4.80—340 pp.

No Nukes: Everyone's Guide to Nuclear Power *by Anna Gyorgy and Friends:* The comprehensive nuclear power handbook, with everything from what it is and how it works, to how to fight it; organizational lessons and strategies. Guide to resources, people, organizations, nuclear and solar terms.
Available: February, 1978 $5.25—256 pp.

Unorthodox Marxism *by Michael Albert and Robin Hahnel:* A critique of orthodox Marxist economics prefaces a new approach to societal reproduction and socialist revolution in the United States. Includes a proposal for a socialist model suitable to the needs and potentialities of the United States.
Available: February, 1978 $4.80—350 pp.

Between Labor and Capital: The Professional and Managerial Class *edited by Pat Walker:* A collection of essay on class relations in the United States. Focuses on the interface between professionals/managers and blue collar workers. Lead article by Barbara and John Ehrenreich.
Available: March, 1978 $4.80—220 pp.

What's Wrong With The American Economy? *by The Institute for Labor Education and Research:* A primer for working people, this book looks at American capitalism in the twentieth century. Based on three years of popular economics courses for rank and file union members and other working people.
Available: March, 1978 $5.00—350 pp.

Crisis in the Working Class *by John McDermott:* Today's obsolete labor movement; collectivized capital; a seven class society; a captive working class; working class socialism; and organizations proposals.
Available: March, 1978 $4.80—350 pp.

REPRINTS

Strike! *by Jeremy Brecher:* A classic account of American labor as a social movement. A new preface by the author draws out the implications for working class organization and action today.
Available: Now $4.95—320 pp.

Common Sense for Hard Times *by Jeremy Brecher and Tim Costello:* Interviews with workers throughout the country and extensive historical research provide the basis for this popularly written analysis of modern times.
Available: Now $4.80—277 pp.